This journal belongs to:

Blessed Assurance

Blessed Assurance

A Devotional Journal for Fruitful Living

Jennifer Flanders

PRESCOTT PUBLISHING
Tyler, Texas

Scripture references marked NASB are taken from THE NEW AMERICAN STANDARD BIBLE ®, Copyright ©1960, 1962, 1963, 1968, 1971, 1972, 1973, 1975, 1977, 1995 by the Lockman Foundation. Used by permission.

Scripture references marked NIV are taken from THE HOLY BIBLE, NEW INTERNATIONAL VERSION ®. Copyright ©1973, 1978, 1984 by International Bible Society.

Scripture references marked ESV are taken from THE HOLY BIBLE, ENGLISH STANDARD VERSION ®. Copyright © 2001 by Crossway Bibles, a publishing ministry of Good News Publishers.

Scripture references marked GWT are taken from GOD'S WORD® TRANSLATION of THE HOLY BIBLE, © 1995 by God's Word to the Nations. Used by permission of Baker Publishing Group.

Scripture references marked NLT are taken from THE HOLY BIBLE, NEW LIVING TRANSLATION, ©1996, 2004. Used by permission of Tyndale House Publishers, Inc. Wheaton, IL 60189. All rights reserved.

Scripture references marked NKJV are taken from THE HOLY BIBLE, NEW KING JAMES VERSION, ©1982, by Thomas Nelson, Inc.

Scripture references marked KJV are taken from the authorized version of THE KING JAMES HOLY BIBLE.

Scripture references marked NET are taken from the NET (NEW ENGLISH TRANSLATION) BIBLE, ©1996-2006, by Biblical Studies Press, L.L.C. http://netbible.com. Used with permission. All rights reserved.

BLESSED ASSURANCE: A DEVOTIONAL JOURNAL FOR FRUITFUL LIVING
Copyright ©2020 by Jennifer Flanders. www.flandersfamily.info

The vast majority of clip art in this book is from a set of 9 CDs my husband bought me back in 1996 called Masterclips 101,000 Premium Images Collection. This was long before I started blogging or writing or publishing anything, and I hadn't the foggiest idea what I'd ever do with such a thing — but I held onto it, just in case, and now I use it all the time!

Additional images (and permission to use them in this publication) were obtained by purchasing a premium membership to The Graphics Fairy (members.thegraphicsfairy.com). I also found a few public domain images at openclipart.org, olddesignshop.com, and freevintageart.com.

All rights reserved. No part of this book may be used or reproduced in any manner whatsoever without written permission except in the case of brief quotations embodied in critical articles and reviews. For information, please address Prescott Publishing, 3668 Southwood Dr, Tyler, TX 75707. http://prescottpublishing.org

ISBN: 978-1-938945-39-7

Dedication

To Lydia, Gwen,
Ellen, Charlotte Rose,
and all the other granddaughters
who will come after them

Contents

Introduction 11

Passion & Purity 13

Gracious Words 27

Walking in Truth 41

Showing Mercy 53

Hopes & Dreams 65

All Loves Excelling 77

Joyful Hearts 89

Peace of Mind 103

Prayers for Patience 119

Acts of Kindness 133

Gifts of Goodness 149

Forever Faithful 167

Gentle Strength 181

Self-Control 197

A Quiet Confidence 211

Freedom of Choice 227

Introduction

God calls Christians to bear spiritual fruit. He intends for our lives to reflect His character to a watching world. This devotional journal explores what such fruit looks like in the lives of those who've put their hope and trust in God.

I pray these pages will prod you to think about the characteristics God says should be evident in the life of every mature Chrisitian. Namely,the the fruit of the Spirit: Love, Joy, Peace, Patience, Kindness, Goodness, Faithfulness, Gentleness, and Self-Control. I've also included chapters on Hope, Grace, Truth, Purity, Confidence, and Mercy, as well as an examination of the choices we make and where they lead us.

There is no right or wrong way to complete this journal. You may use the blank spaces to record thoughts, compose poetry, set goals, write prayers, paste photographs, paint pictures, draw sketches, make lists, tape mementos— or a combination of any or all of the above. You don't need to finish the pages in order, so feel free to skip around.

This book contains several word studies that will help you dig deeply into each topic. You'll also find writing prompts in the form of questions. Consider these carefully: Am I bearing fruit as God desires? Have I remained in the vine, drawing nourishment from God's Word and communicating with Him daily in prayer? Is the fruit I'm producing ripe, well-formed, and abundant?

I believe the best place to find answers to such questions is through God's Word, so you'll find lots of Bible verses scattered throughout these pages, along with beautiful vintage artwork.

The title of the book is taken from an old hymn I love, which you will find printed on the next page. Life is often full of uncertainties. Isn't it a blessed assurance to know that the God who began a good work in your heart and life will be faithful to see that work to completion?

May His richest blessings be yours,
Jennifer Flanders

Blessed Assurance
by Earnest J. Ford

Blessed assurance, Jesus is mine!
O, what a foretaste of glory divine!
Heir of salvation, purchase of God,
Born of His Spirit, washed in His blood.

Perfect submission, perfect delight,
Visions of rapture now burst on my sight;
Angels, descending, bring from above
Echoes of mercy, whispers of love.

Perfect submission, all is at rest,
I in my Savior am happy and blessed,
Watching and waiting, looking above,
Filled with His goodness, lost in His love.

This is my story, this is my song,
Praising my Savior all the day long.
This is my story, this is my song,
Praising my Savior all the day long.

Passion & Purity

What kind of example am I?

"Let no one look down on your youthfulness,
but rather in speech, conduct, love, faith and purity,
show yourself an example of those who believe."

- 1 Timothy 4:12, NASB

Be an example to all believers

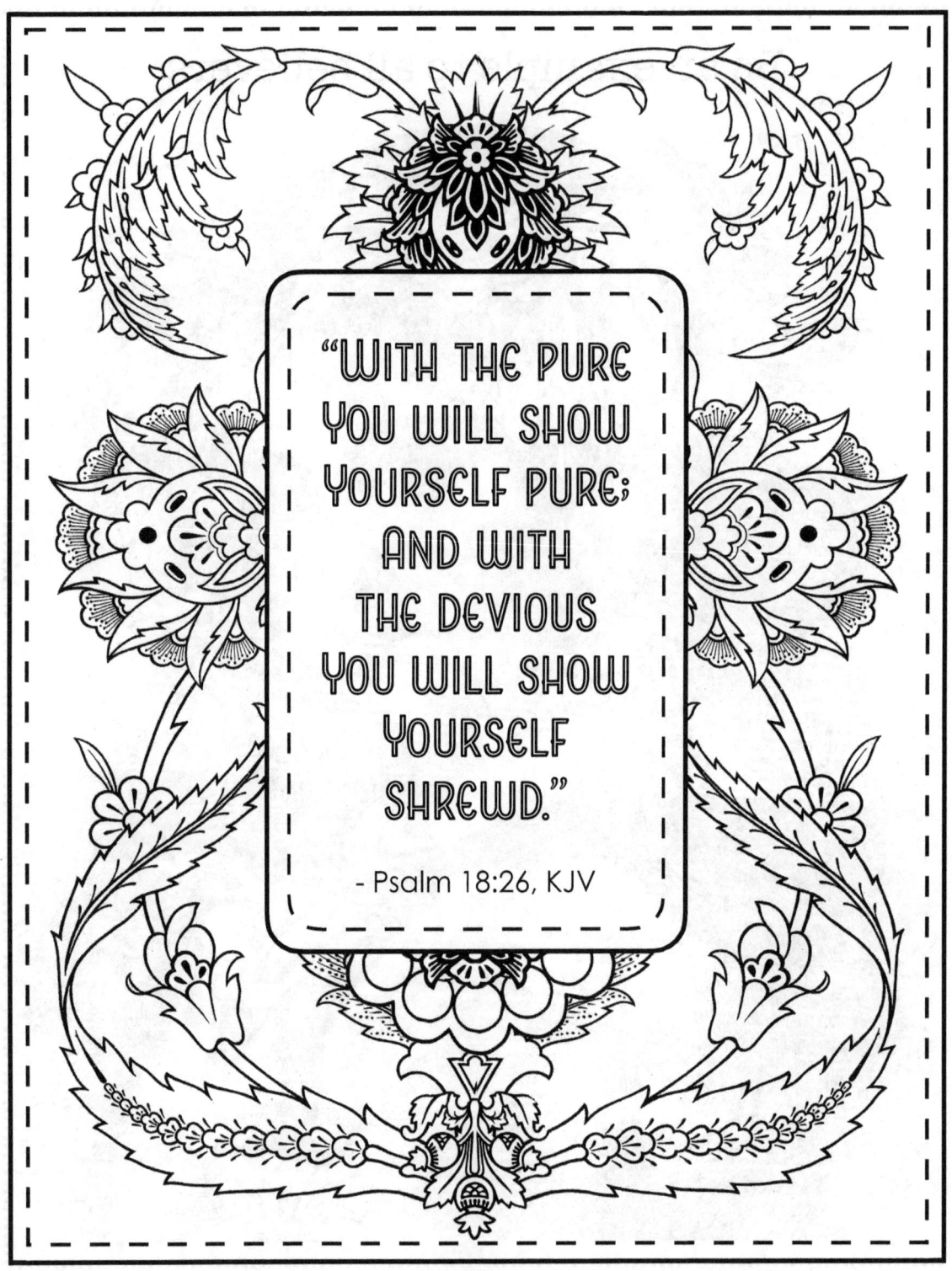

Psalm 119:9

Proverbs 22:11

Titus 2:7

1 Timothy 1:5

1 John 3:3

James 1:27

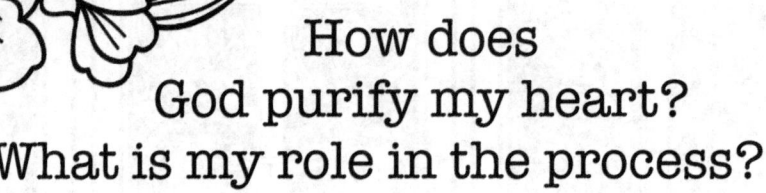

How does
God purify my heart?
What is my role in the process?

"Draw near to God and He will draw near to you.
Cleanse your hands, you sinners;
and purify your hearts, you double-minded."

- James 4:8, NASB

But the wisdom from above is **first pure**, then peaceable, gentle, reasonable, **full of mercy** and good fruits, **unwavering**, without hypocrisy.

- James 3:17
NASB

If Purity is the rudder that guides our ship, Then Passion is the wind that fills our sails.

Where will my passion take me?

"For a remnant of my people will spread out from Jerusalem, a group of survivors from Mount Zion. The passionate commitment of the LORD of Heaven's Armies will make this happen!"

- 2 Kings 19:31, NLT

"The LORD detests the thoughts of the wicked,
but gracious words are pure in His sight."

- Proverbs 15:26

Gracious Words

What the Bible says about grace:

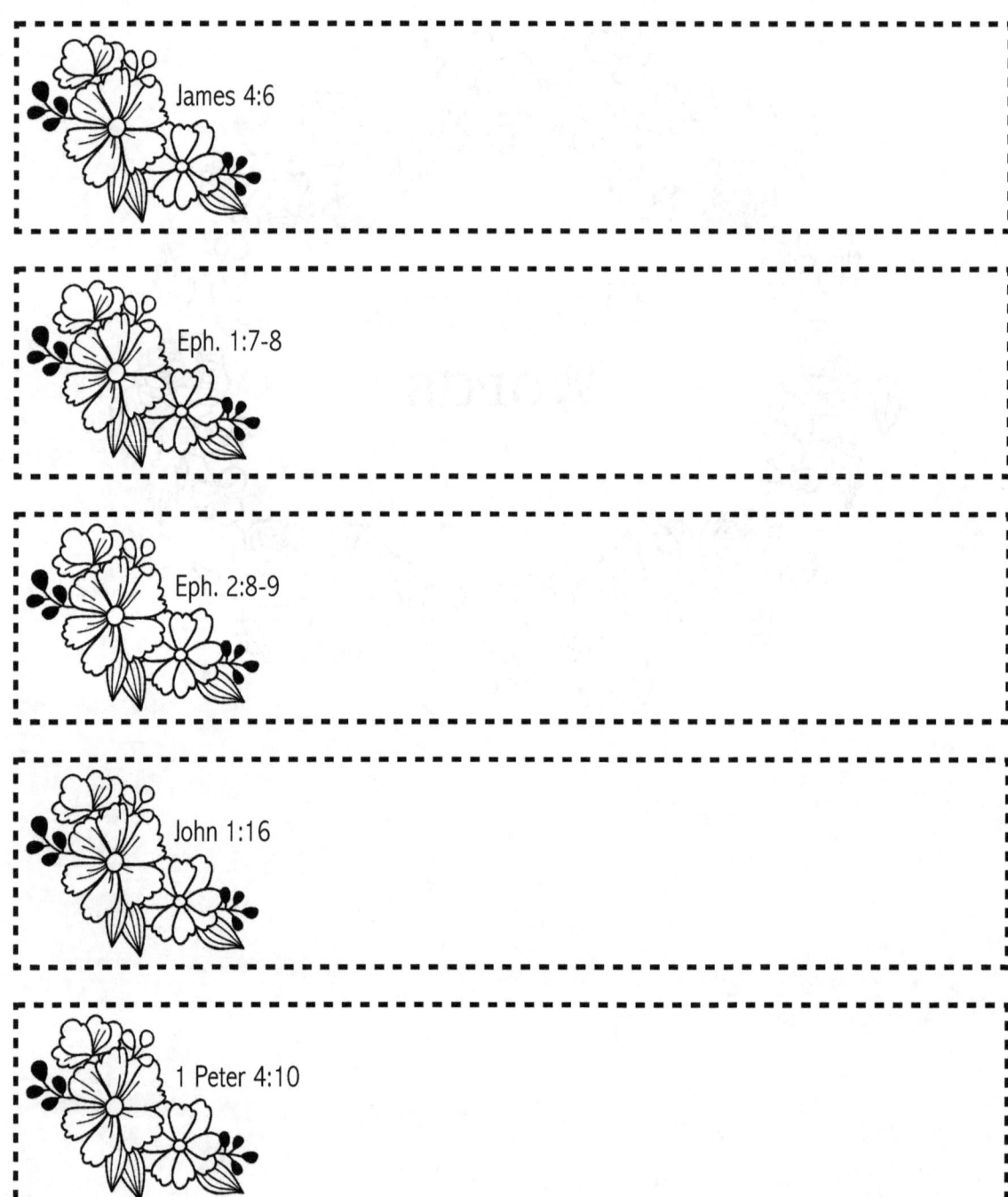

- James 4:6
- Eph. 1:7-8
- Eph. 2:8-9
- John 1:16
- 1 Peter 4:10

What do grace-filled words sound like?

"Let your conversation be always full of grace, seasoned with salt, so that you may know how to answer everyone."

- Colossians 4:6, NIV

Gracious words are heartfelt & persuasive

"The heart of the wise instructs his mouth
And adds persuasiveness to his lips."

- Proverbs 16:23, NASB

Gracious words are wise and kind

"She opens her mouth with wisdom,
And on her tongue *is* the law of kindness."

- Proverbs 31:26, NKJV

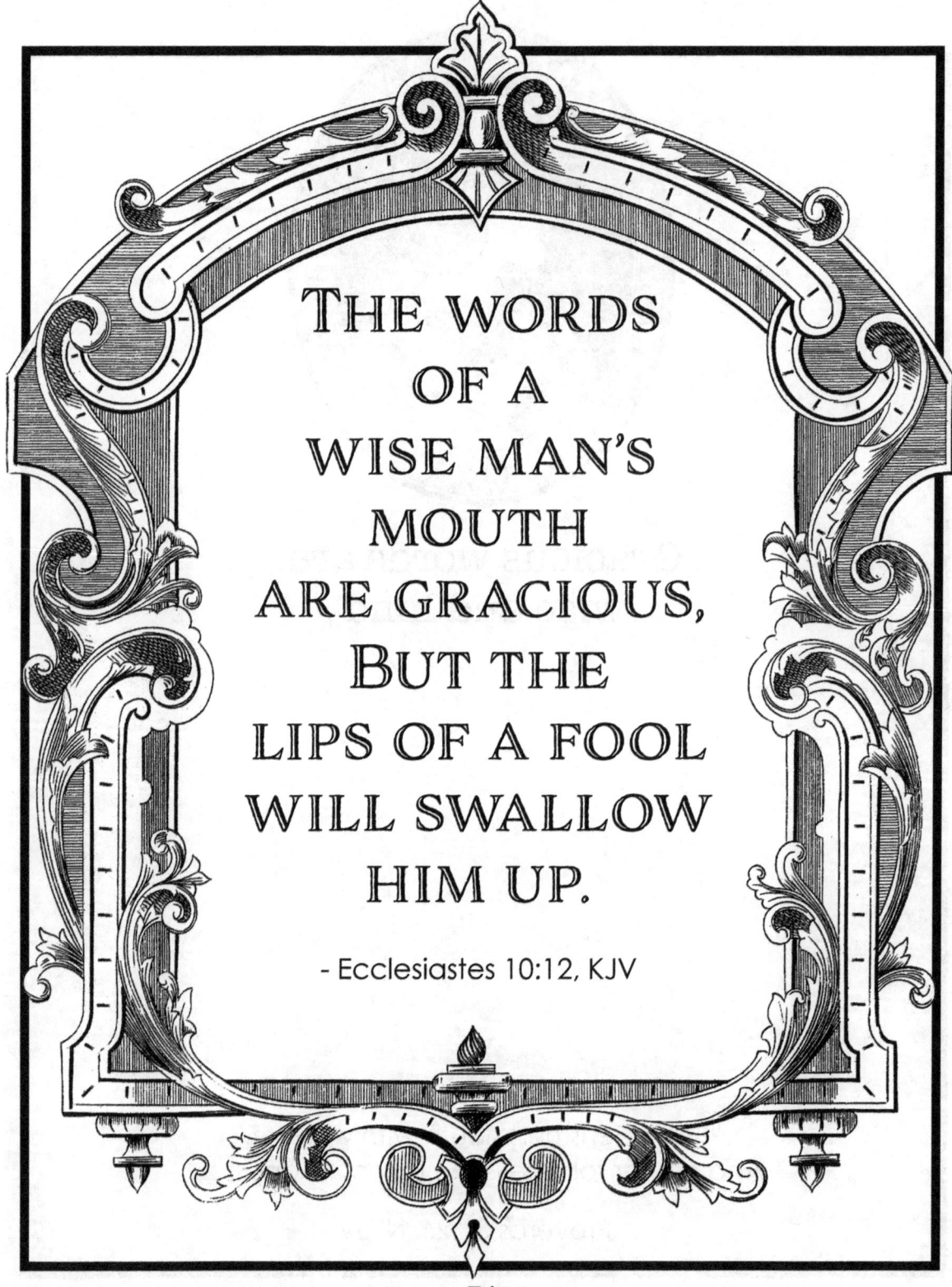

What the Bible says about our words:

Let my written words be gracious, as well...

"My tongue is the pen of a skillful writer."

- Psalm 45:1, NIV

full of wisdom, kindness & encouragement.

"Dear friends,
although I have been eager
to write to you
about our common salvation,
I now feel compelled instead
to write to encourage you
to contend earnestly for the faith
that was once for all
entrusted to the saints."

- Jude 1:3, NET

Reading Challenge

Pick a book that fits
each of the following descriptions,
then check off the box once you've finished reading it:

- ☐ read an **A**ward-winning book
- ☐ read a **B**iography
- ☐ read a book set in another **C**ountry
- ☐ read a book about a **D**og
- ☐ read a book set in another **E**ra
- ☐ read a work of **F**antasy **F**iction
- ☐ read a **G**raphic novel
- ☐ read a book of **H**istorical fiction
- ☐ read an **I**nstruction manual
- ☐ read a **J**oke book
- ☐ read a book written for **K**ids
- ☐ read a **L**ove story
- ☐ read book made into a **M**ovie
- ☐ read a **N**on-fiction book
- ☐ read about the great **O**utdoors
- ☐ read a book of **P**oetry
- ☐ read a book of **Q**uestions
- ☐ read a book about **R**oyalty
- ☐ read some **S**hakespeare
- ☐ read a book on **T**heology
- ☐ read a book about an **U**nderdog
- ☐ read a tale of **V**alor & **V**irtue
- ☐ read a book on **W**orld travel
- ☐ read an e**X**citing adventure story
- ☐ re-read one of **Y**our favorites
- ☐ read about a **Z**oo animal

*Today a reader,
tomorrow a leader.*

— Margaret Fuller

"He who loves purity of heart *And has* grace on his lips,
The king *will be* his friend."

- Proverbs 22:11, NKJV

Walking in Truth

Psalm 1:1-6

Blessed *is* the man who walks not in the counsel
of the ungodly,
nor stands in the way of sinners,
nor sits in the seat of the scornful.
But his delight
is in the law of
the LORD;
and in His law does he meditate day and night.

He shall be like a Tree
planted
by the rivers of water,
that brings forth its fruit in its season;
whose leaf also shall not wither;
and whatever he does shall prosper.

The ungodly *are* not so:
but *are* like the chaff which the wind drives away.
Therefore the ungodly shall not stand
in the judgment,
nor sinners in the congregation of the righteous.
For the
LORD knows the way of the righteous:
but the way of the ungodly
shall perish."

God, give me wise friends
who walk in the truth

"Whoever walks with the wise becomes wise,
but the companion of fools will suffer harm."

- Proverbs 13:20, ESV

Unto Thee, O LORD, do I lift up my soul. O my God, I **trust in Thee**: let me not be ashamed, let not mine enemies triumph over me. Yea, let none that wait on Thee be ashamed: let them be ashamed which transgress without cause. **Show me Thy ways**, O LORD; **teach me Thy paths. Lead me in Thy truth**, and teach me: for Thou art the God of my salvation; on Thee do I wait all the day. Remember, O Lord Thy tender mercies and Thy lovingkindnesses; for they have been ever of old. Remember not the sins of my youth, nor my transgressions: according to Thy mercy remember Thou me for Thy goodness' sake, O LORD. Good and **upright** is the LORD: therefore will he teach sinners in the way. The meek will he guide in judgment: and the meek **will He teach** His way. All the paths of the Lord are mercy and truth unto such as keep

Psalm 25

What the Bible says about walking in truth:

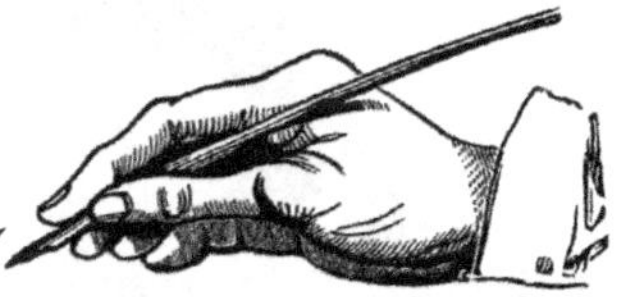

1 John 1:6-7

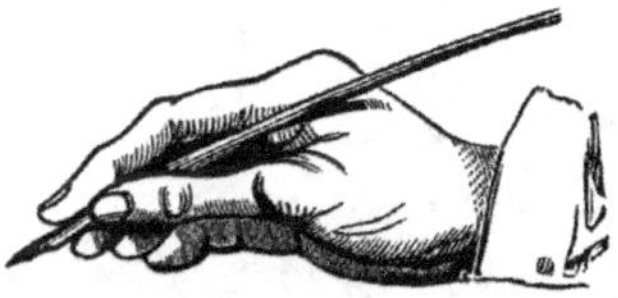

Psalm 15:1-2

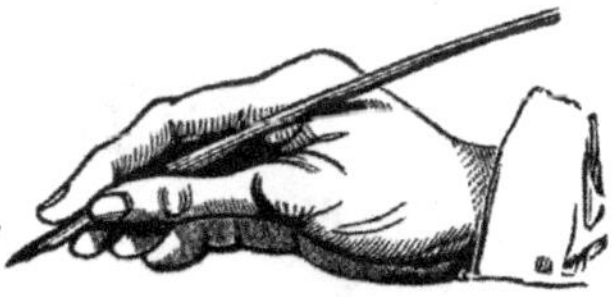

Psalm 84:11

Proverbs 10:9

Psalm 86:11

3 John 1:4

"All wise ladies grow — From little girls like me"

The Truth lights our way

"Thy word *is* a lamp unto my feet, and a light unto my path."

- Psalm 119:105, KJV

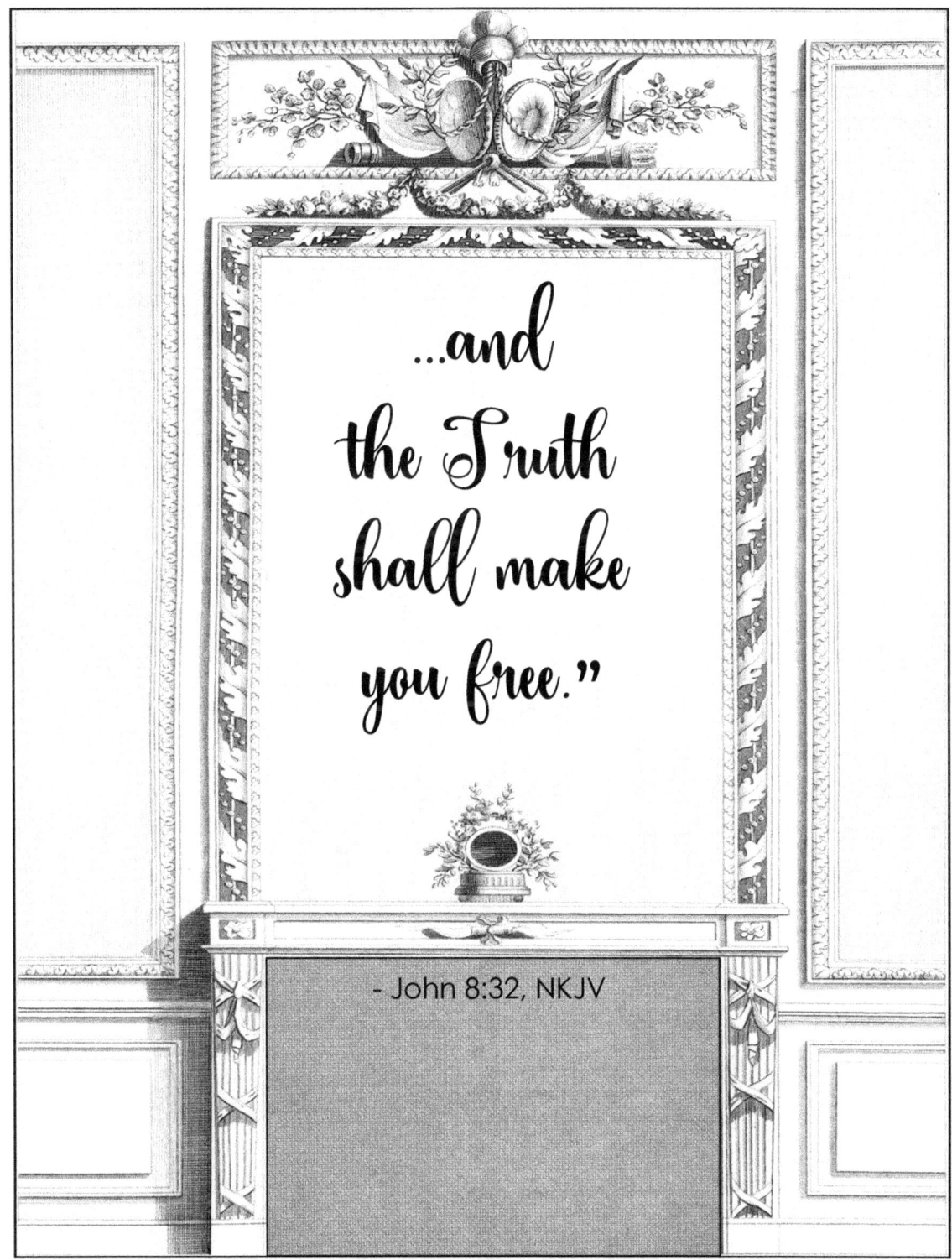

"...and the Truth shall make you free."

- John 8:32, NKJV

"Set them apart in the truth; Your word is truth."

- John 17:17, NET

Showing Mercy

God lavishes mercy on me.
How can I extend it to others?

"Be merciful, just as your Father is merciful."

- Luke 6:36, NIV

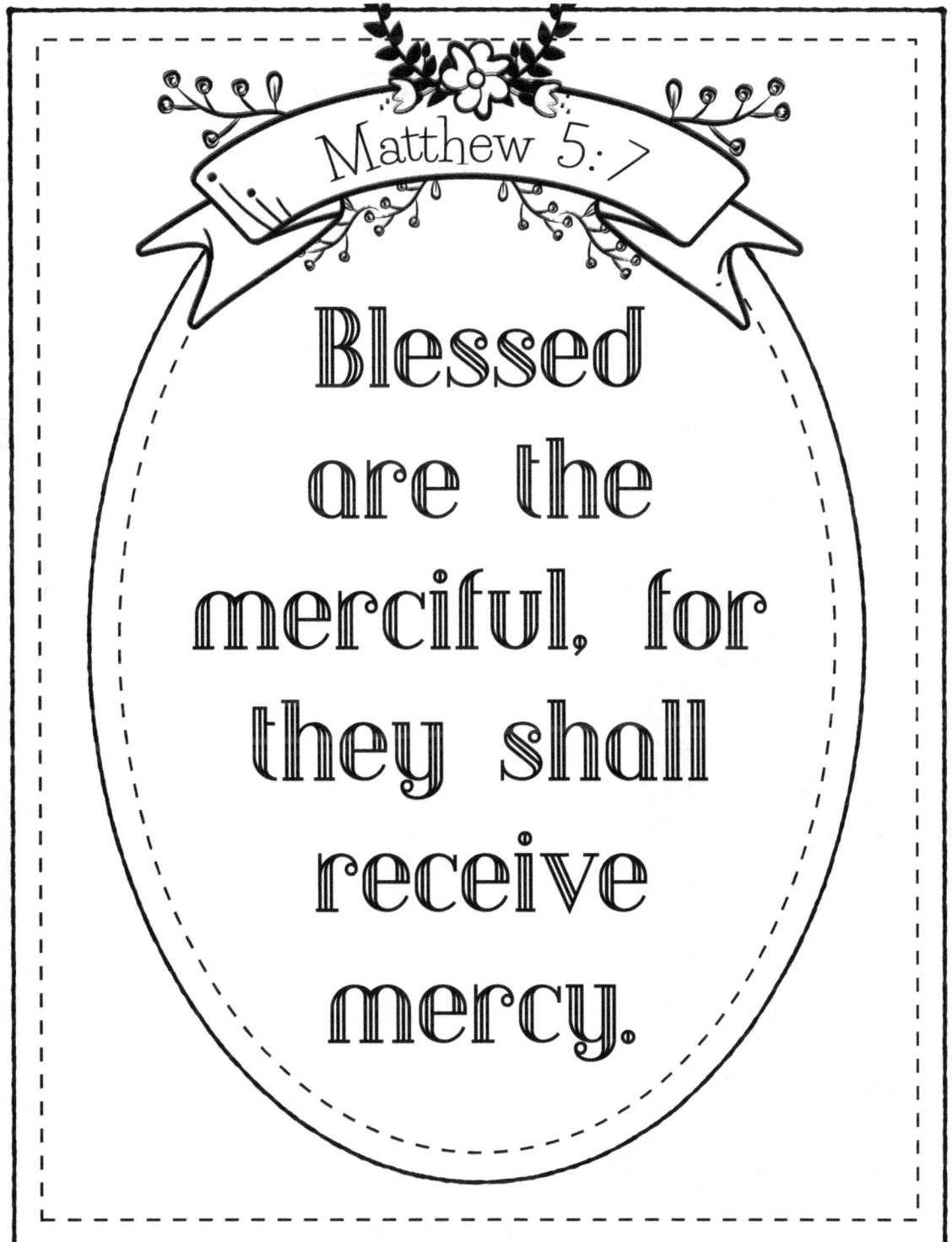

Wait upon the Lord

"Keep yourselves in God's love
as you wait for the mercy
of our Lord Jesus Christ
to bring you to eternal life."

- Jude 1:21, NIV

Walk in humility

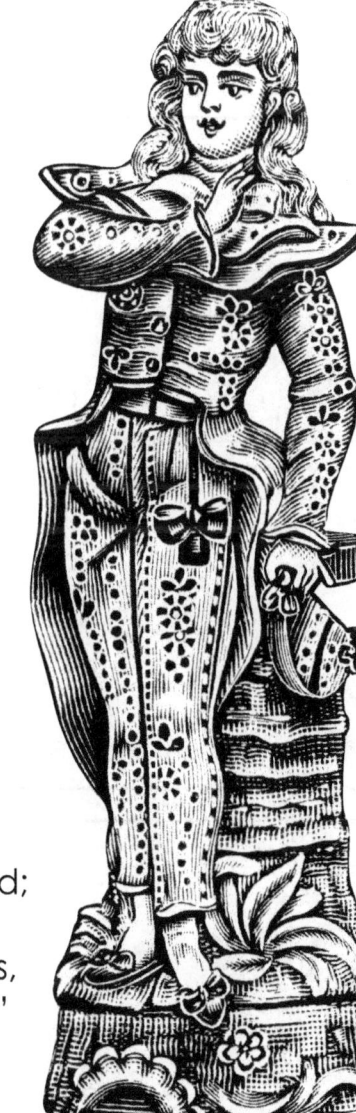

"He has told you, O man, what is good;
And what does the LORD require of
you but to do justice, to love kindness,
And to walk humbly with your God?"

- Micah 6:8, NIV

What the Bible says about mercy:

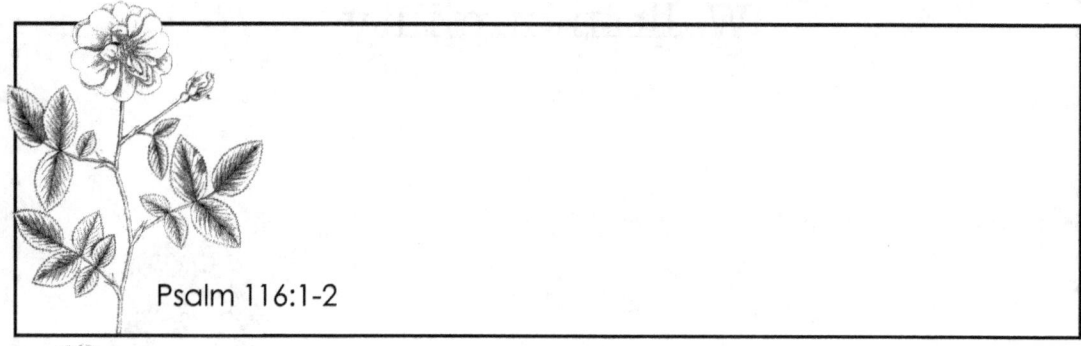

Psalm 116:1-2

Psalm 119:132-133

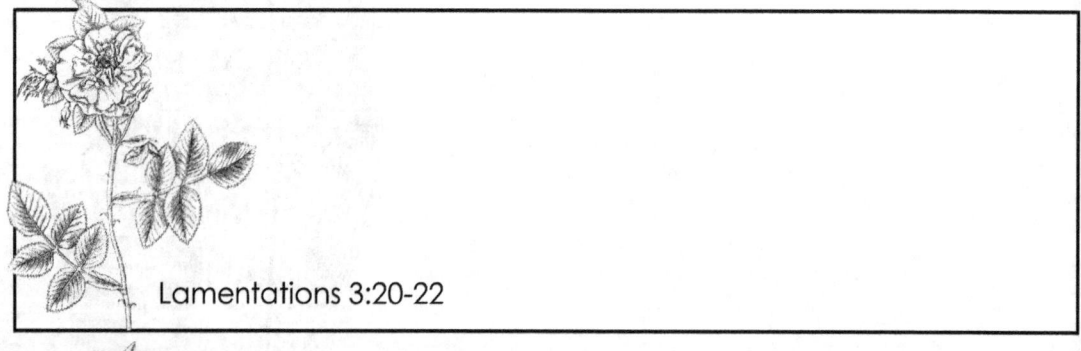

Lamentations 3:20-22

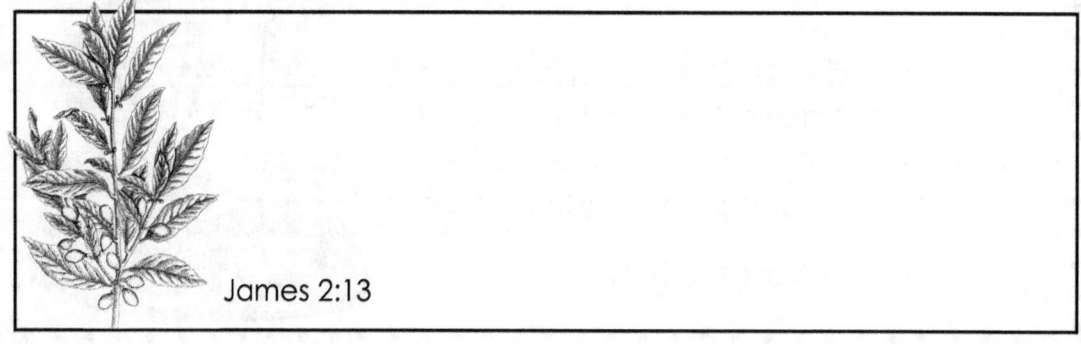

James 2:13

Our God is rich in mercy

"But because of
His great love for us, God,
Who is rich in mercy,
made us alive with Christ,
even when we were dead
in our trespasses.
It is by grace
you have
been saved!"

- Ephesians 2:4-5

Let us be merciful
to both man and beast

"A righteous man has pity for the lives of his cattle;
but the bowels of the ungodly are unmerciful."

- Proverbs 12:10

Let us show mercy to those in need

"If anyone has material possessions and sees a brother or sister in need but has no pity on them, how can the love of God be in that person?"

- 1 John 3:17, NIV

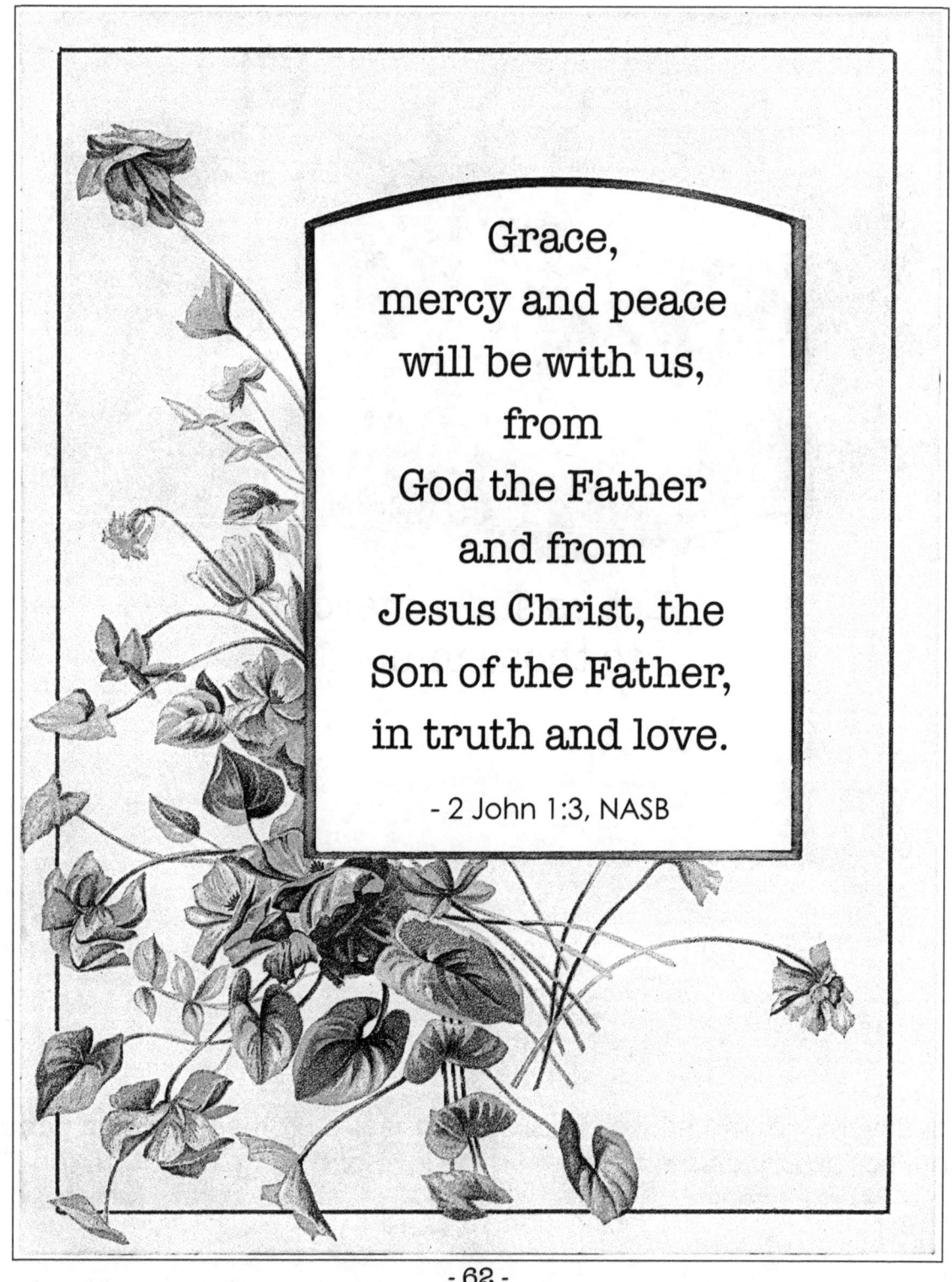

> Grace, mercy and peace will be with us, from God the Father and from Jesus Christ, the Son of the Father, in truth and love.
>
> - 2 John 1:3, NASB

Answer me,
LORD,
out of
the goodness
of Your love;
in Your
great mercy
turn to me.

- Psalm 69:16, NIV

"For I desire mercy and not sacrifice,
And the knowledge of God more than burnt offerings."

- Hosea 6:6, KJV

Hopes & Dreams

Steadfast in Hope

"And let us hold unwaveringly to the hope that we confess, for the one who made the promise is trustworthy."

- Hebrews 10:23, NET

May the God of Hope Fill You With All Joy and Peace.

— Romans 15:13 —

Hope gives us courage

"Therefore, since we have such a hope, we are very bold."

- 2 Corinthians 3:12, NIV

For in this hope
we were saved.
But hope that is seen
is no hope at all.
Who hopes for
what
they
already
have?

Romans 8:24
NIV

Titus 2:13

Ephesians 4:2-4

Colossians 1:4-5

Romans 15:13

"Blessed be the God and Father
of our Lord Jesus Christ,
who according to His great mercy
has caused us to be born again
to a living hope
through the resurrection
of Jesus Christ from the dead,
to obtain an inheritance
which is imperishable & undefiled
and will not fade away."

- 1 Peter 1:3-4, NASB

Our hope includes eternal life, a home in heaven, and what else?

"Israel, put your hope in the LORD,
for with the LORD is unfailing love and with him is full redemption."

- Psalm 130:7, NIV

Don't keep your dreams caged up inside you

"For the needy are not permanently ignored, the hopes of the oppressed are not forever dashed."

- Psalm 9:18, NET

Set them free and let your hopes take wing

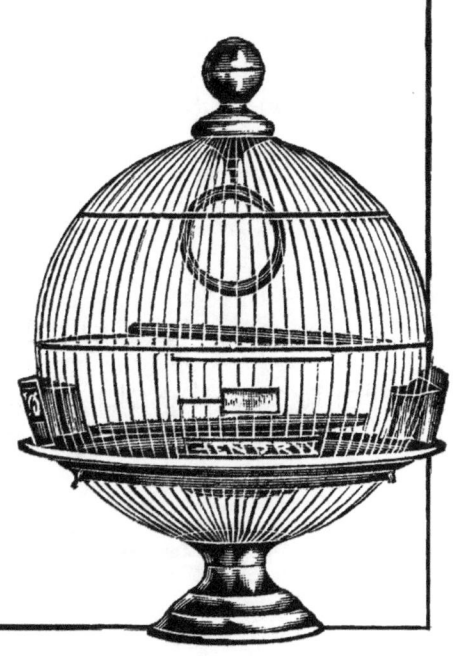

"Surely there is a future,
And your hope will not be cut off."

- Proverbs 23:18, NASB

"For I know the plans I have for you," declares the LORD, "plans to prosper you & not to harm you, plans to give you hope & a future."

- Jeremiah 29:11, NIV

All Loves Excelling

Luke 6:32   1 John 4:18

1 John 4:16

1 John 4:20

"Love the Lord your God with all your heart and with all your soul and with all your mind and with all your strength."

- Mark 12:30, NIV

Nothing greater

"And now these three remain: faith, hope and love.
But the greatest of these is love."

- 1 Corinthians 13:13, NIV

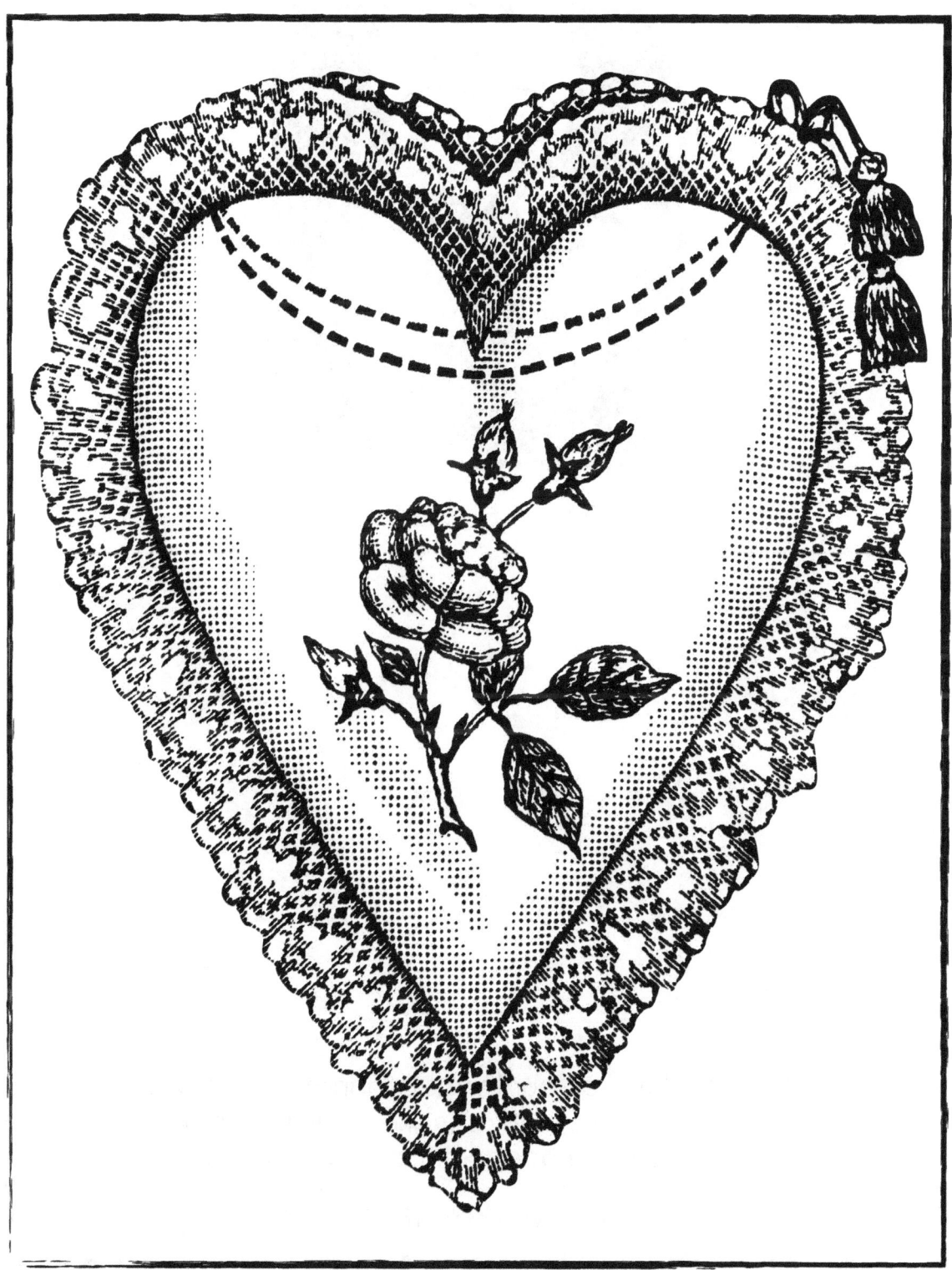

Love One Another

"There are three or four things I cannot understand:
How eagles fly so high or snakes crawl on rocks,
how ships sail the ocean or people fall in love."

- Proverbs 30:18-19

How do we recognize true love?

True love is easy to spot. Just look for the following traits:

U	N	D	E	R	S	T	A	N	D	I	N	G	X	Q	W	A	S	T
K	E	F	A	I	T	H	F	U	L	O	Y	A	L	B	M	D	F	R
S	T	E	A	G	F	E	A	C	A	R	I	N	G	G	E	I	D	U
N	D	T	R	H	U	L	U	O	O	D	L	E	O	V	R	L	N	S
R	L	I	N	T	D	B	S	N	O	U	P	M	R	I	C	E	I	T
E	U	C	R	E	R	M	S	T	F	O	R	G	I	V	I	N	G	W
G	F	U	N	O	H	U	M	E	P	A	D	T	O	G	F	I	N	O
N	E	B	T	U	B	H	S	N	W	T	K	N	E	O	U	E	I	R
A	T	T	E	S	E	E	U	T	A	H	I	U	E	O	L	L	T	T
O	A	N	X	L	L	P	A	T	I	E	N	T	S	D	U	N	F	H
T	R	E	W	F	I	J	U	S	T	N	D	H	S	F	F	S	I	Y
W	G	T	L	P	P	E	G	R	G	L	G	A	Y	U	R	C	L	P
O	W	E	C	O	N	S	V	A	E	T	I	O	K	L	E	E	P	A
L	S	U	P	P	O	R	T	I	V	E	J	I	B	R	Y	K	U	T
S	H	E	L	P	F	U	L	L	N	C	O	N	S	T	A	N	T	Y
E	V	E	R	L	A	S	T	I	N	G	P	E	A	C	R	E	J	O
S	T	E	A	D	Y	E	T	A	N	O	I	S	S	A	P	M	O	C

patient	believing	trustworthy	slow to anger
kind	helpful	merciful	forgiving
trusting	constant	loyal	joyful
content	good	uplifting	righteous
humble	understanding	compassionate	pure
courteous	faithful	prayerful	just
selfless	true	everlasting	supportive
grateful	caring	warm	steady

Love God, Love Others

"Beloved, if God so loved us,
we also ought to love one another."

- 1 John 4:11, NASB

"This is how we know what love is:
Jesus Christ laid down his life for us."

- 1 John 3:16, NIV

Joyful Hearts

"Whatever you do, work at it wholeheartedly as though you were doing it for the Lord and not merely for people."

- Colossians 3:23, ISV

"For you were called to freedom, brothers. Only do not use your freedom as an opportunity for the flesh, but through love serve one another."

- Galatians 5:13, ESV

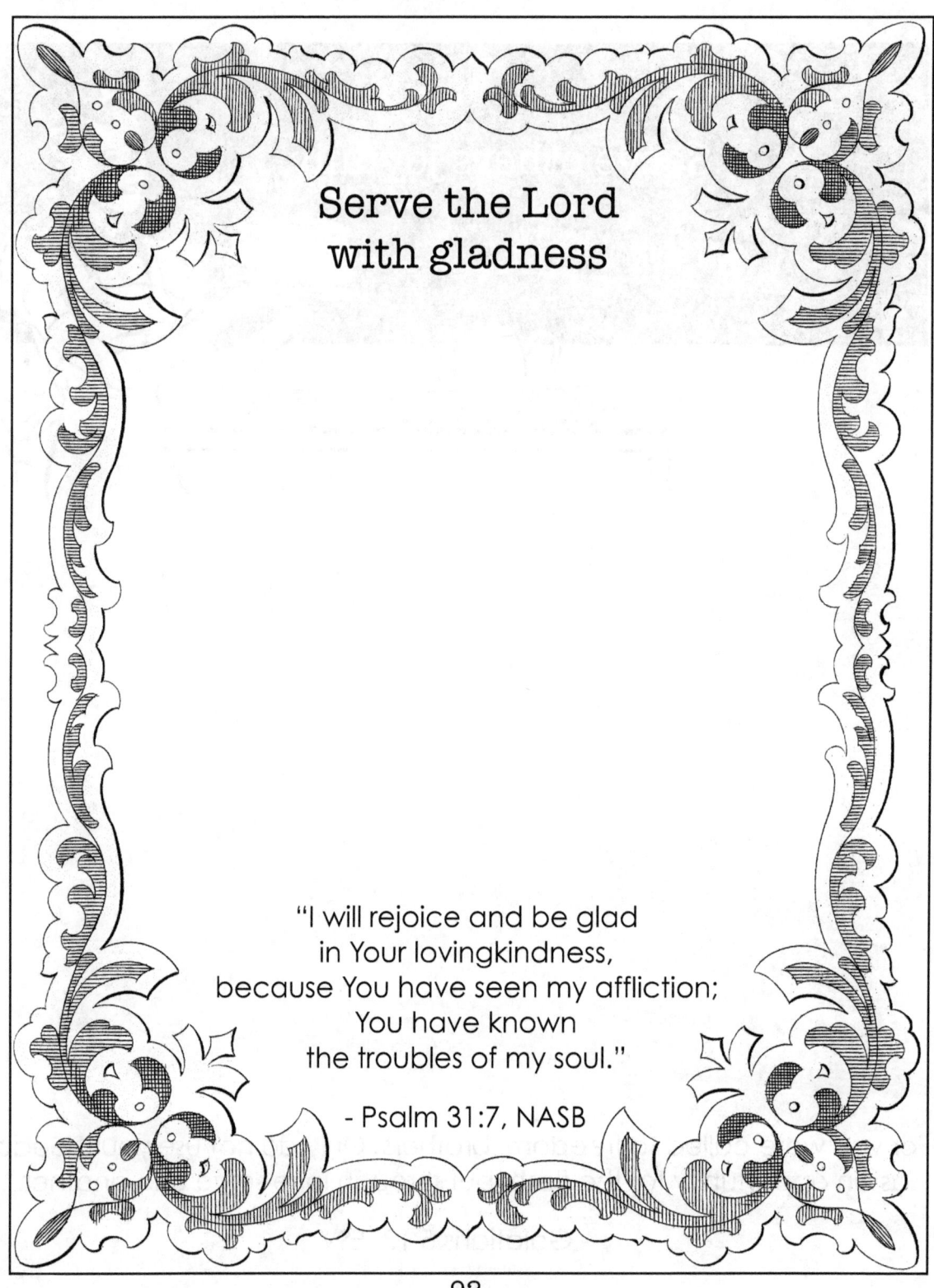

Serve the Lord with gladness

"I will rejoice and be glad
in Your lovingkindness,
because You have seen my affliction;
You have known
the troubles of my soul."

- Psalm 31:7, NASB

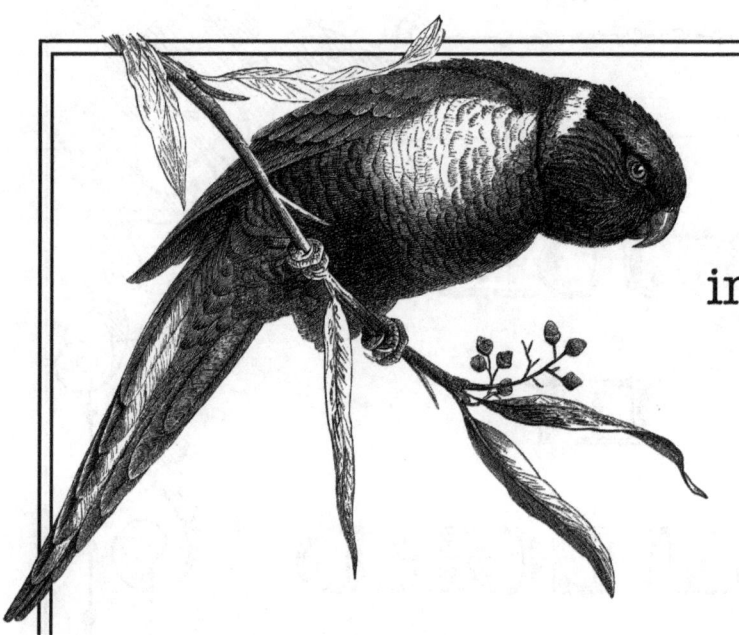

Joy comes in the morning

"For His anger is but for a moment, His favor is for a lifetime;
Weeping may last for the night,
But a shout of joy comes in the morning."

- Psalm 30:5, NASB

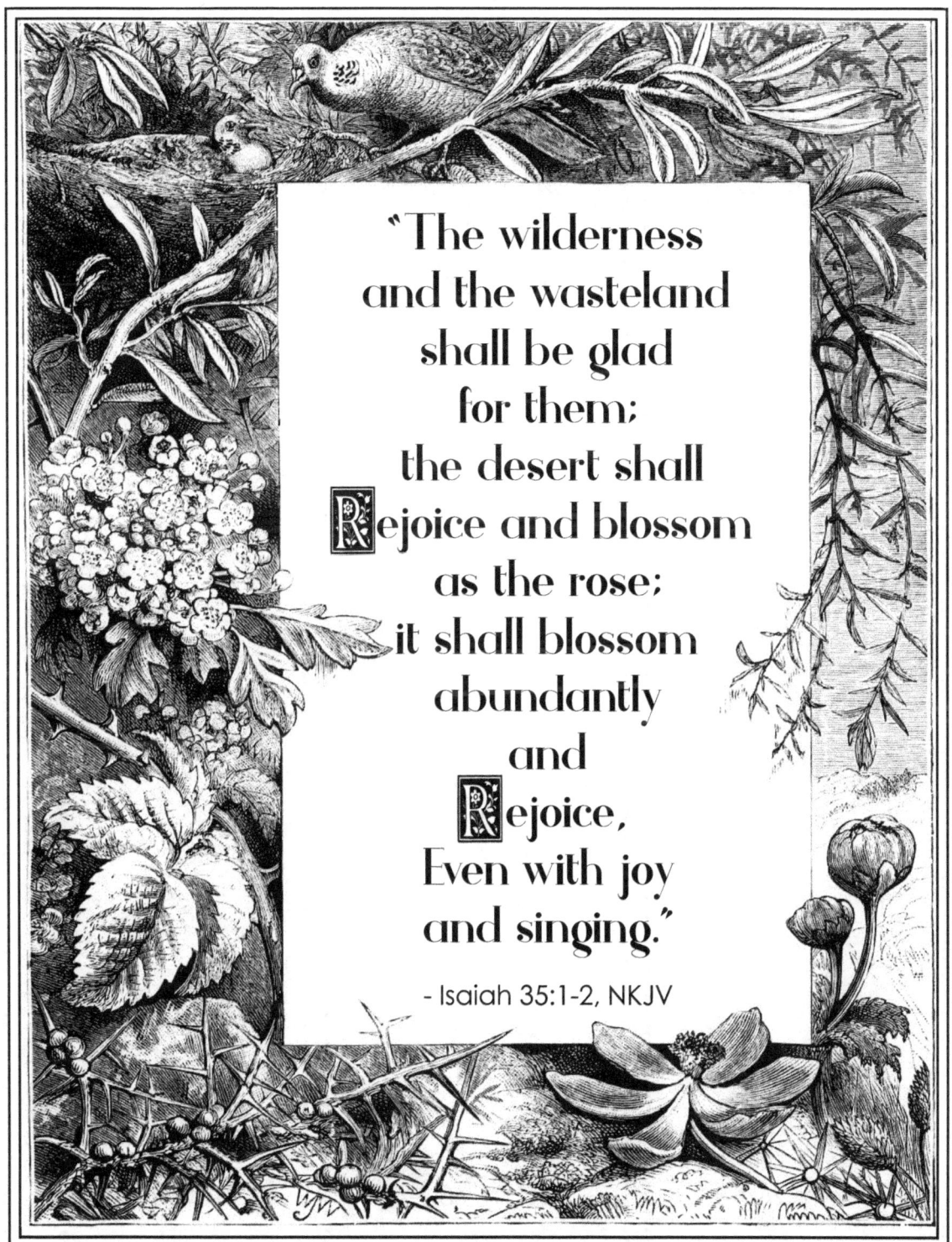

"The wilderness and the wasteland shall be glad for them; the desert shall Rejoice and blossom as the rose; it shall blossom abundantly and Rejoice, Even with joy and singing."

- Isaiah 35:1-2, NKJV

"Joyful" means to be "filled with joy."

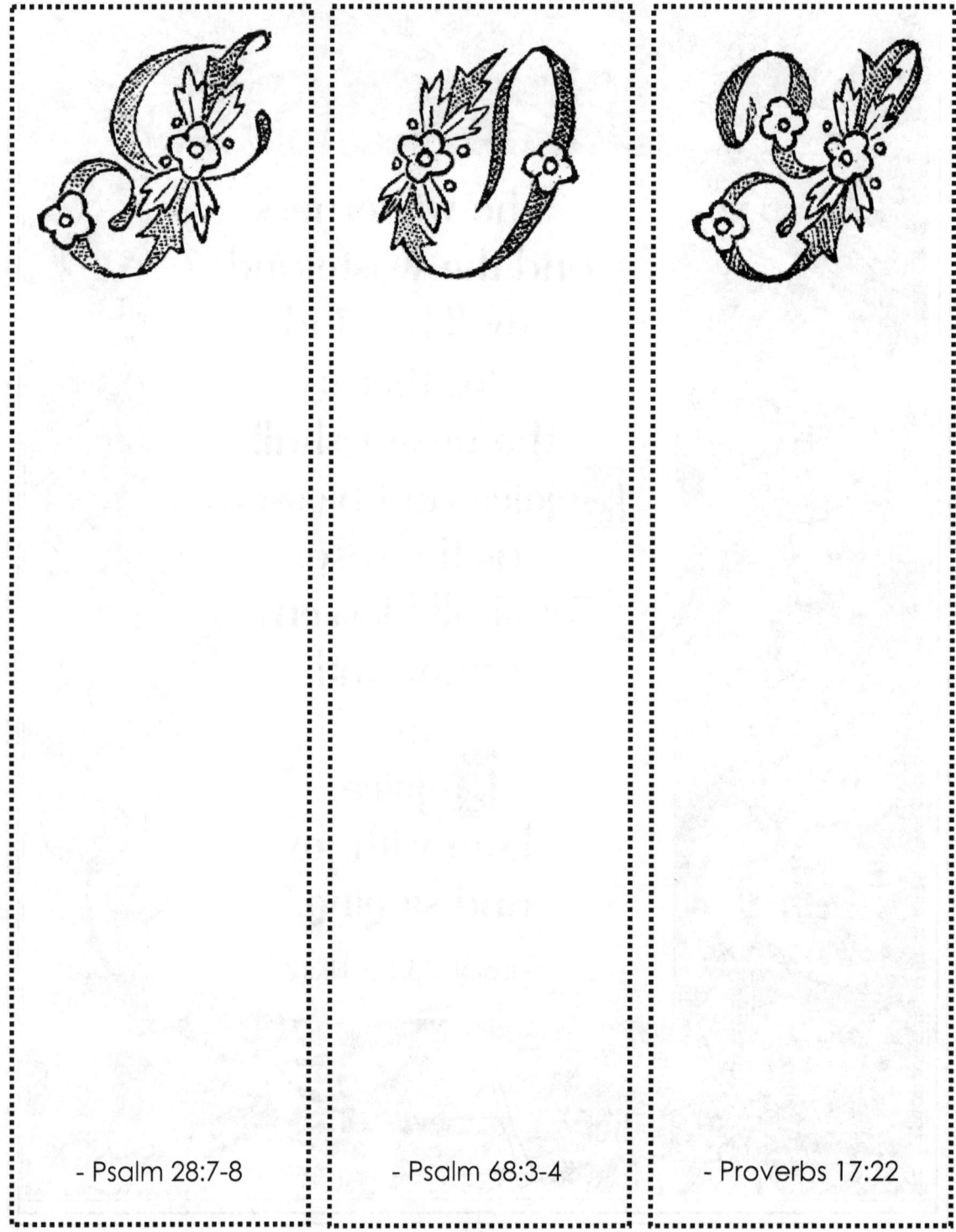

- Psalm 28:7-8

- Psalm 68:3-4

- Proverbs 17:22

Is "joyful" a fitting description of me?

- Proverbs 15:13

- Psalm 100:1-2

- Nehemiah 8:10

Rejoice in the LORD

"Yet I will rejoice in the LORD, I will be joyful in God my Savior. The Sovereign LORD is my strength; He makes my feet like the feet of a deer, He enables me to tread on the heights."

- Habakkuk 3:18-19, NIV

Shout for Joy!

"Then will the lame leap like a deer,
and the mute tongue shout for joy. Water will gush forth
in the wilderness and streams in the desert."

- Isaiah 35:6, NIV

How can I cultivate joy in my heart?

"Let those who love the Lord hate evil, for He guards the lives of His faithful ones & delivers them from the hand of the wicked. Light shines on the righteous & joy on the upright in heart. Rejoice in the Lord, you who are righteous & praise His holy name."

- Psalm 97:10-12

What can I do to bring joy to others?

"Make my joy complete by being of the same mind, maintaining the same love, united in spirit, intent on one purpose. Do nothing from selfishness or empty conceit, but with humility of mind regard one another as more important than yourselves."

- Philippians 2:2-3, NASB

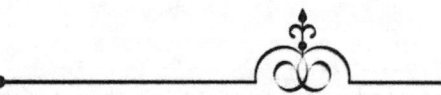

"Be joyful in hope, patient in affliction,
faithful in prayer."

- Romans 12:12, NIV

Peace of Mind

How can I be a peacemaker?

"Blessed are the peacemakers,
for they will be called children of God."

- Matthew 5:9, NIV

How can I live in peace with all?

"If it is possible, as much as depends on you,
live peaceably with all men."

- Romans 12:18, NKJV

I will lie down
and sleep
in peace,
for You alone,
O LORD,
make me dwell
in safety.

Psalm 4:8

Do others see Jesus in me?

"Make every effort to live in peace
with everyone and to be holy;
without holiness
no one will see the Lord."

- Hebrews 12:14
NIV

Does my life please and glorify God?

"When a man's ways are pleasing to the LORD,
He makes even his enemies to be
at peace with him."

- Proverbs 16:7, NASB

Do I love what God loves?

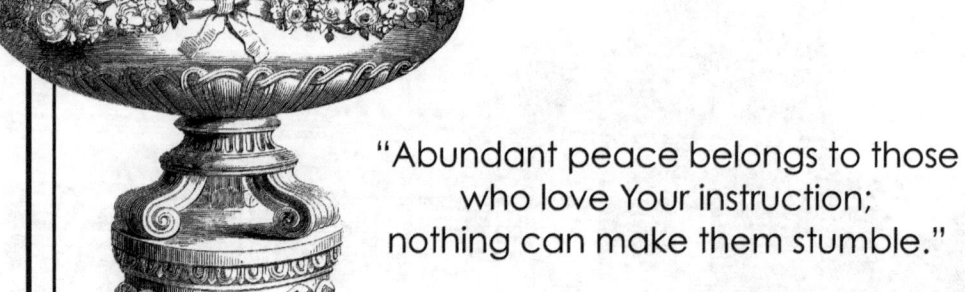

"Abundant peace belongs to those
who love Your instruction;
nothing can make them stumble."

- Psalm 119:165
Berean Study Bible

What the Bible says about peace:

- James 3:17-18

- Hebrews 12:11

- Proverbs 3:1-2

- Mark 9:50

- 1 Thess. 5:12-13

God be with you

"Now may the God of peace be with all of you. Amen."

- Romans 15:33, NET

"Finally, brethren, rejoice, be made complete, be comforted, be like-minded, live in peace; and the God of love and peace will be with you."

- 2 Corinthians 13:11, NASB

Am I more likely
to smile at the future or fret over it?

"She is clothed with strength and dignity,
and she laughs without fear of the future."

- Proverbs 31:25, NLT

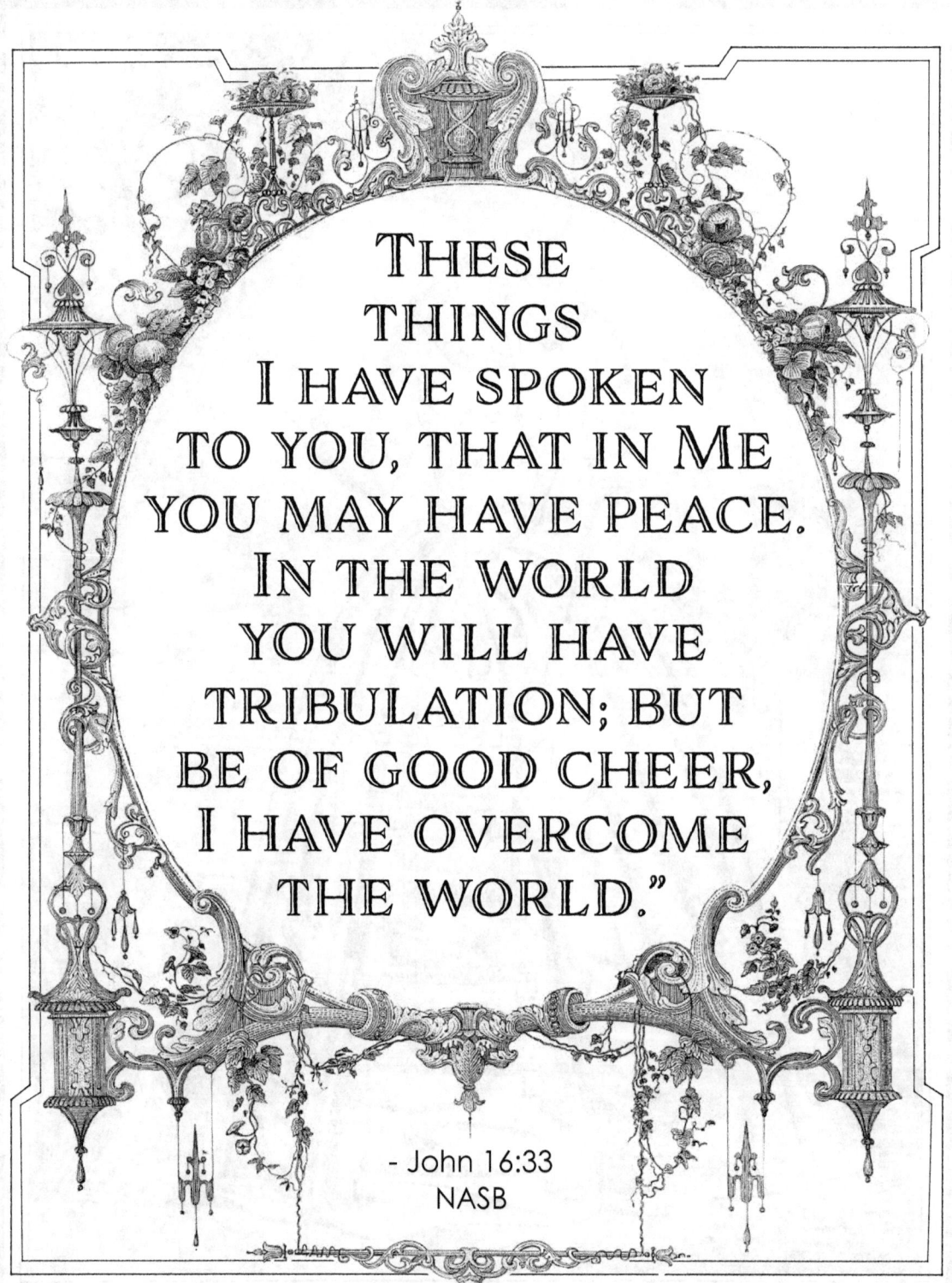

"These things I have spoken to you, that in Me you may have peace. In the world you will have tribulation; but be of good cheer, I have overcome the world."

- John 16:33
NASB

And the peace of God,
which surpasses
all understanding,
will guard your hearts
and minds
through Christ Jesus.

Phil 4:7
NKJV

"Peace I leave with you; My peace I give you. I do not give to you as the world gives. Do not let your hearts be troubled & do not be afraid."

- John 14:27, NIV

Prayers for Patience

"A person's wisdom yields patience; it is to one's glory to overlook an offense."

- Proverbs 19:11, NIV

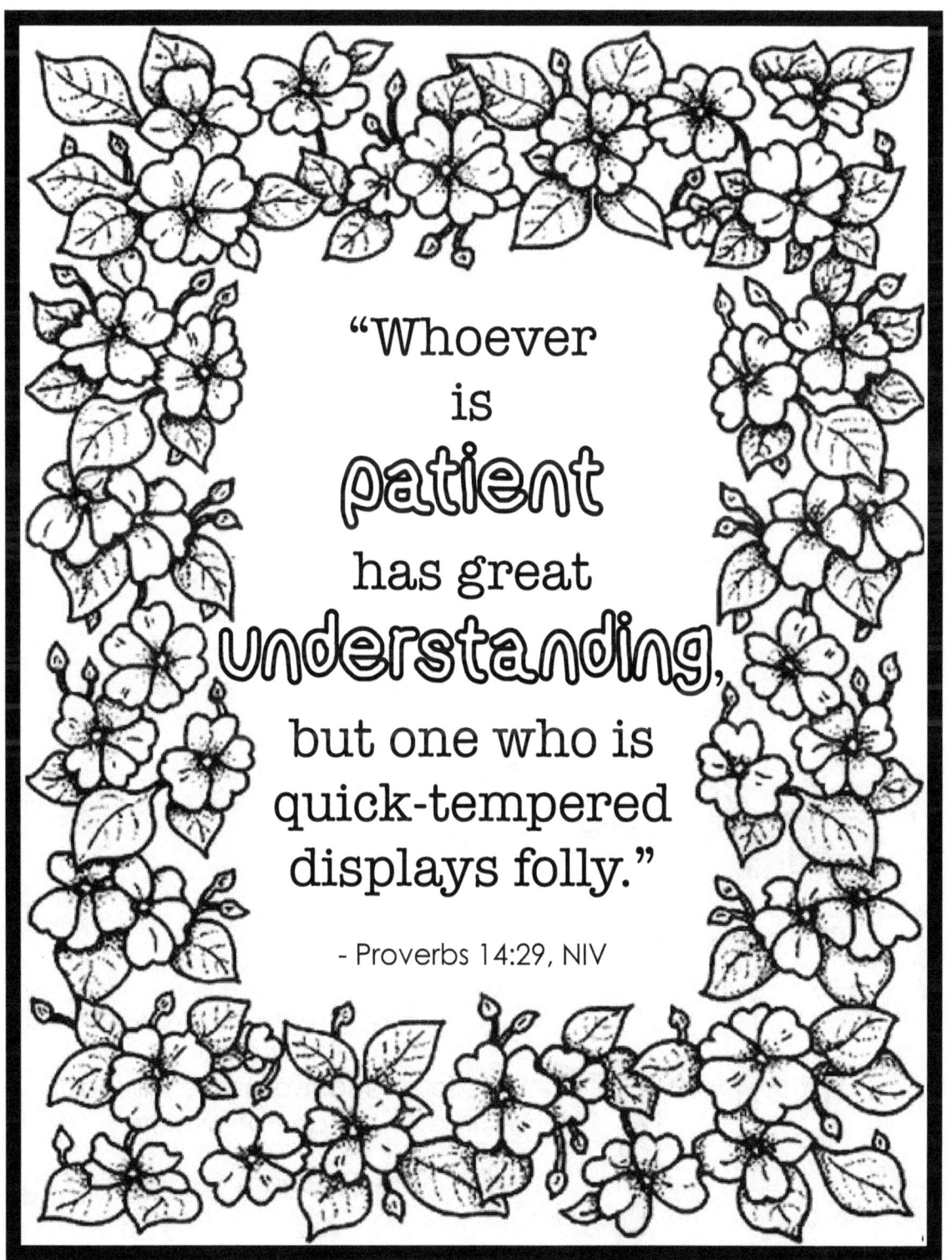

"Whoever is **patient** has great **understanding,** but one who is quick-tempered displays folly."

- Proverbs 14:29, NIV

Am I bearing good fruit?

"And let us not grow weary
of doing good,
for in due season we will reap,
if we do not give up."

- Galatians 6:9, ESV

Am I doing good work?

"For we are God's handiwork,
created in Christ Jesus to do good works,
which God prepared in advance
for us to do."

- Ephesians 2:10, NIV

- James 5:7-8
- Psalm 130:5-6
- Eph. 4:2
- Psalm 40:1-2

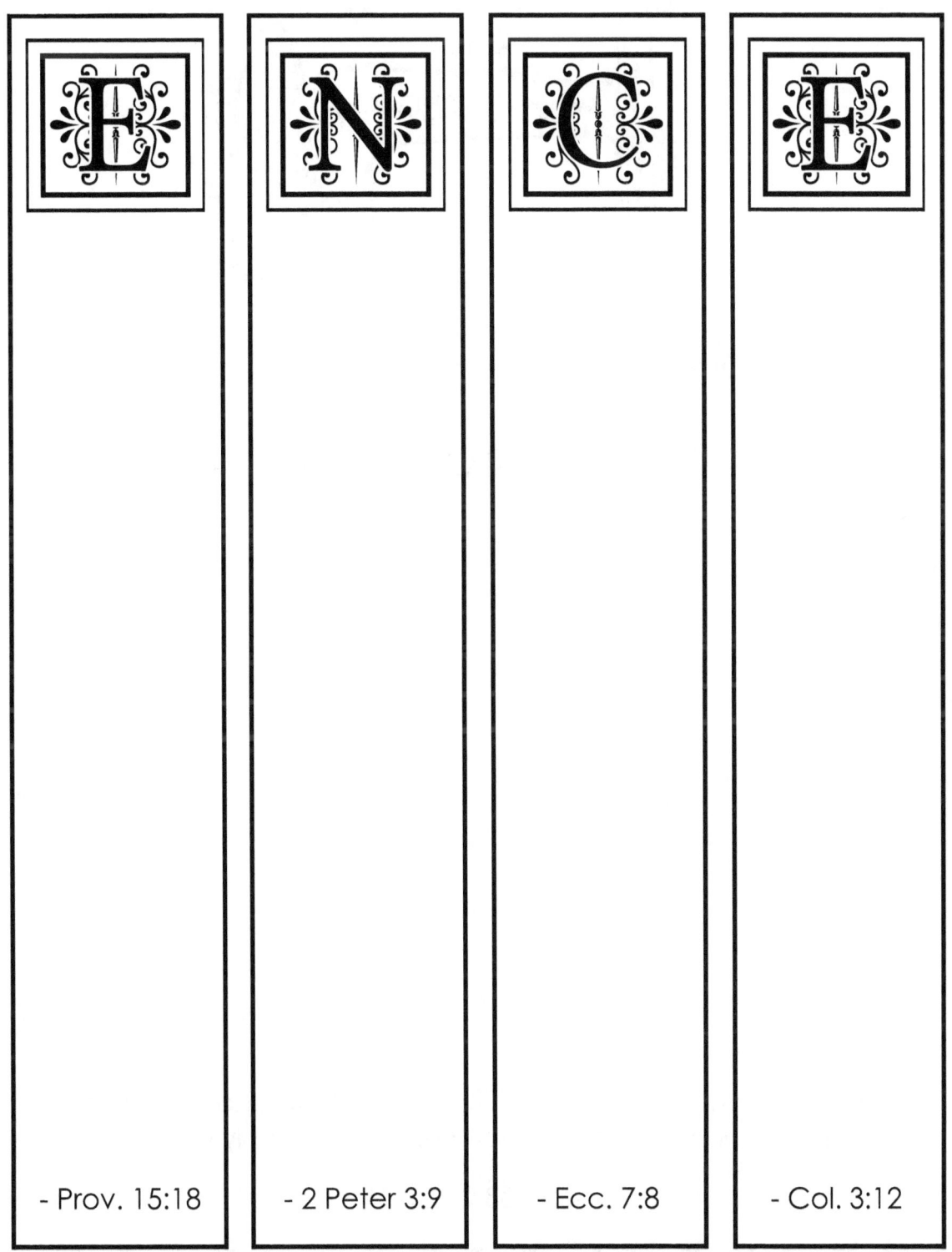

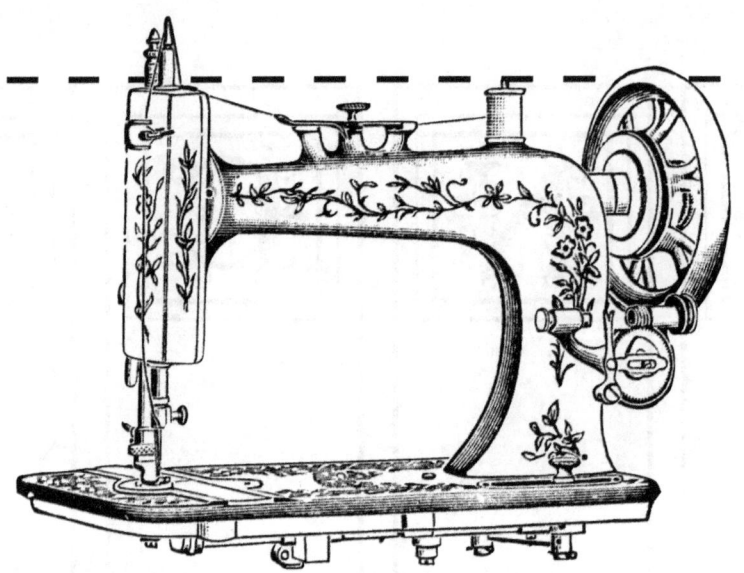

Where do I put my hope & trust?

"We wait in hope for the LORD; He is our help and our shield.
In Him our hearts rejoice, for we trust in His holy name."

- Psalm 33:20-21, NIV

What should I do while I'm waiting on the Lord?

"Wait patiently for the LORD.
Be brave and courageous.
Yes, wait patiently for the LORD."

- Psalm 27:14, NLT

Rev. 2:3 NASB

What does it mean to be steadfast?

"...you have persisted steadfastly, endured much for My name's sake and have not grown weary."

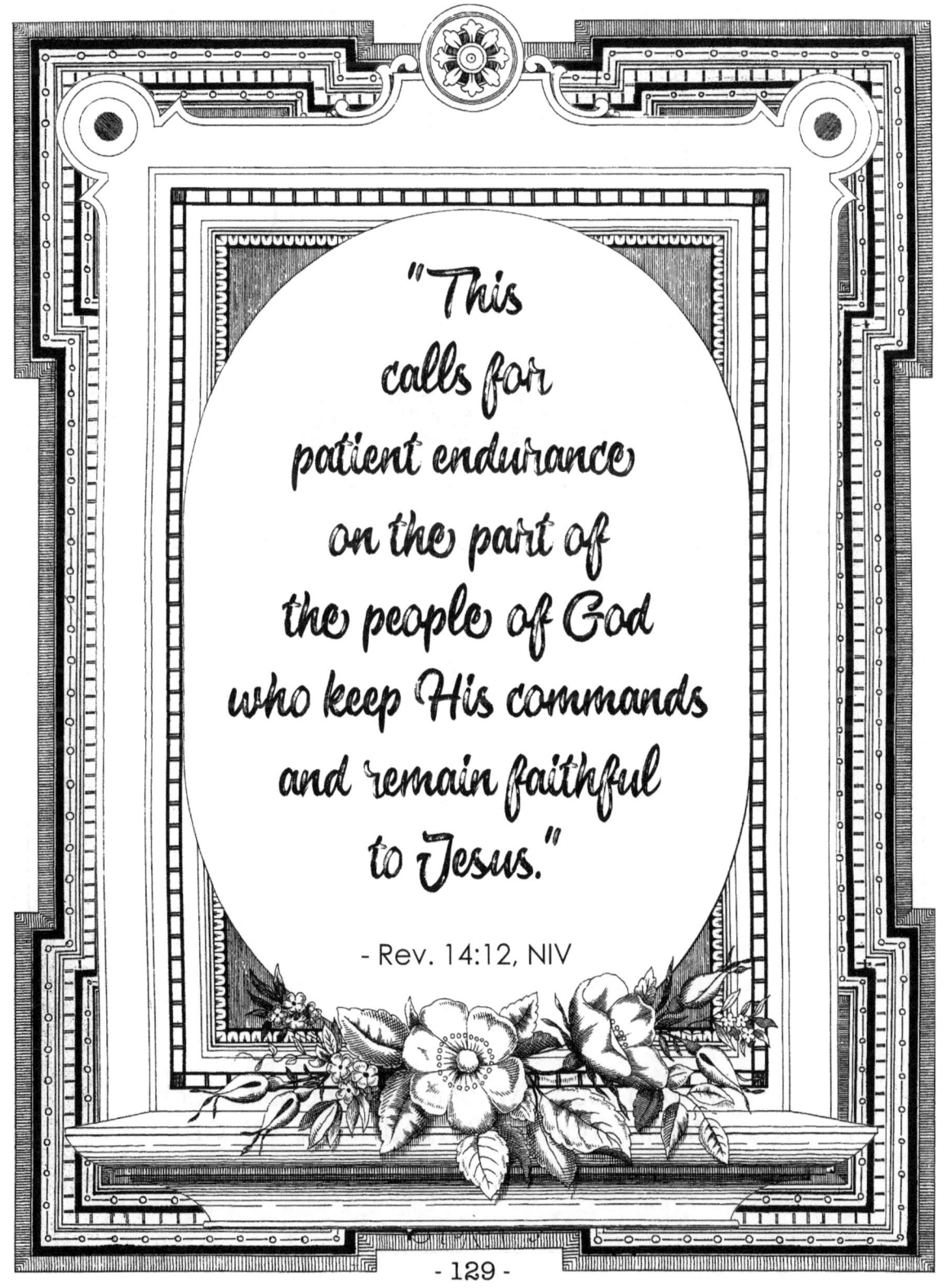

Am I able to endure hardship patiently?

"But if when you do what is right and suffer for it
you patiently endure it, this finds favor with God."

- 1 Peter 2:20, NASB

Do I know how to be still & wait?

"Be still before the LORD and wait patiently for Him."

- Psalm 37:7, NIV

"So that you may live a life worthy of the Lord & please Him
in every way: bearing fruit in every good work,
growing in the knowledge of God,
being strengthened with all power according to His glorious might
so that you may have great endurance and patience."

- Colossians 1:10-11, NIV

Acts of Kindness

Sow Kindness

"Be kind to one another, tender-hearted, forgiving each other, just as God in Christ also has forgiven you."

- Ephesians 4:32, NASB

Reap Joy

"In order that in the coming ages
He might show the incomparable riches of His grace,
expressed in His kindness to us in Christ Jesus."

- Ephesians 2:7, NIV

Wear kindness like a garment

"Therefore, as God's chosen people, holy and dearly loved, clothe yourselves with compassion, kindness, humility, gentleness and patience."

- Colossians 3:12, NIV

What the Bible says about kindness:

Titus 3:4-5

Luke 6:35

1 Corinthians 13:4

2 Chronicles 10:7

Don't you see
how wonderfully kind,
tolerant, and patient
God is with you?
Does this mean nothing to you?
Can't you see
that His kindness is intended
to turn you
from your sin?

- Romans 2:4
NLT

How can I share His kindness with others?

Be thoughtful toward others

"Treat others the same way you want them to treat you."

- Luke 6:31, NASB

Be kind to those in need

"He will have compassion on the poor and needy, and the lives of the needy he will save."

- Psalm 72:13, NASB

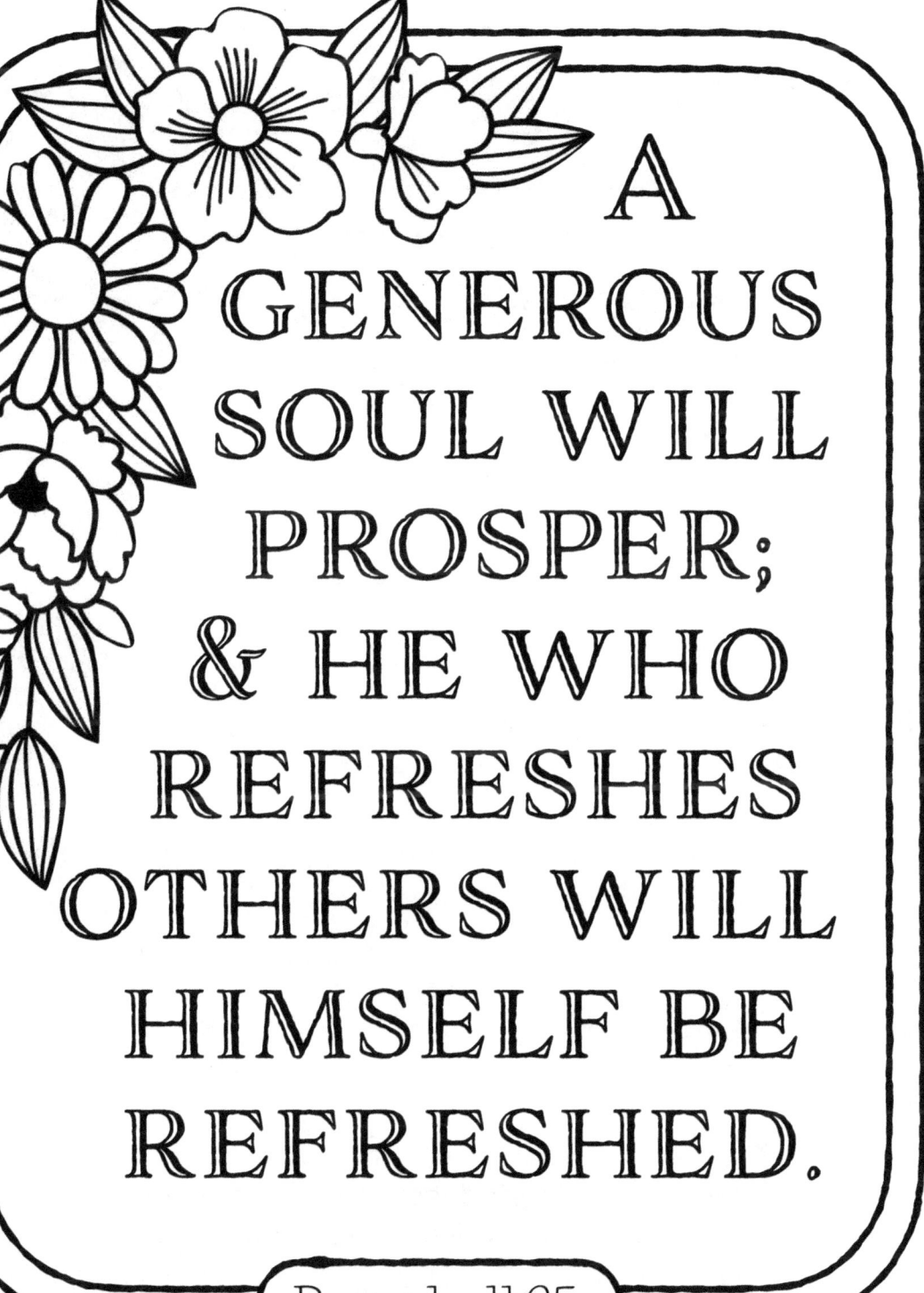

Ever before my eyes

"For your lovingkindness is before my eyes: and I have walked in Your truth."

- Psalm 26:3, NKJV

Better than life

"Because Your lovingkindness is better than life,
My lips will praise You."

- Psalm 63:3, NASB

Am I kind without fail?

"The LORD appeared to us
in the past, saying:
'I have loved you
with an everlasting love;
I have drawn you with unfailing kindness.'"

- Jeremiah 31:3, NIV

"I will tell of the kindnesses of the LORD, the deeds for which He is to be praised, according to all the LORD has done for us."

- Isaiah 63:7, NIV

Gifts of Goodness

What kind of fruit do I produce?

"For there is no good tree which produces bad fruit,
nor, on the other hand, a bad tree which produces good fruit.
For each tree is known by its own fruit."

- Luke 6:43-44, NASB

"The good person
out of the good treasure of his heart produces good,
and the evil person out of his evil treasure produces evil,
for out of the abundance of the heart his mouth speaks.

- Luke 6:45, ESV

God is good

"The LORD *is* good to all: and His tender mercies *are* over all His works."

- Psalm 145:9, KJV

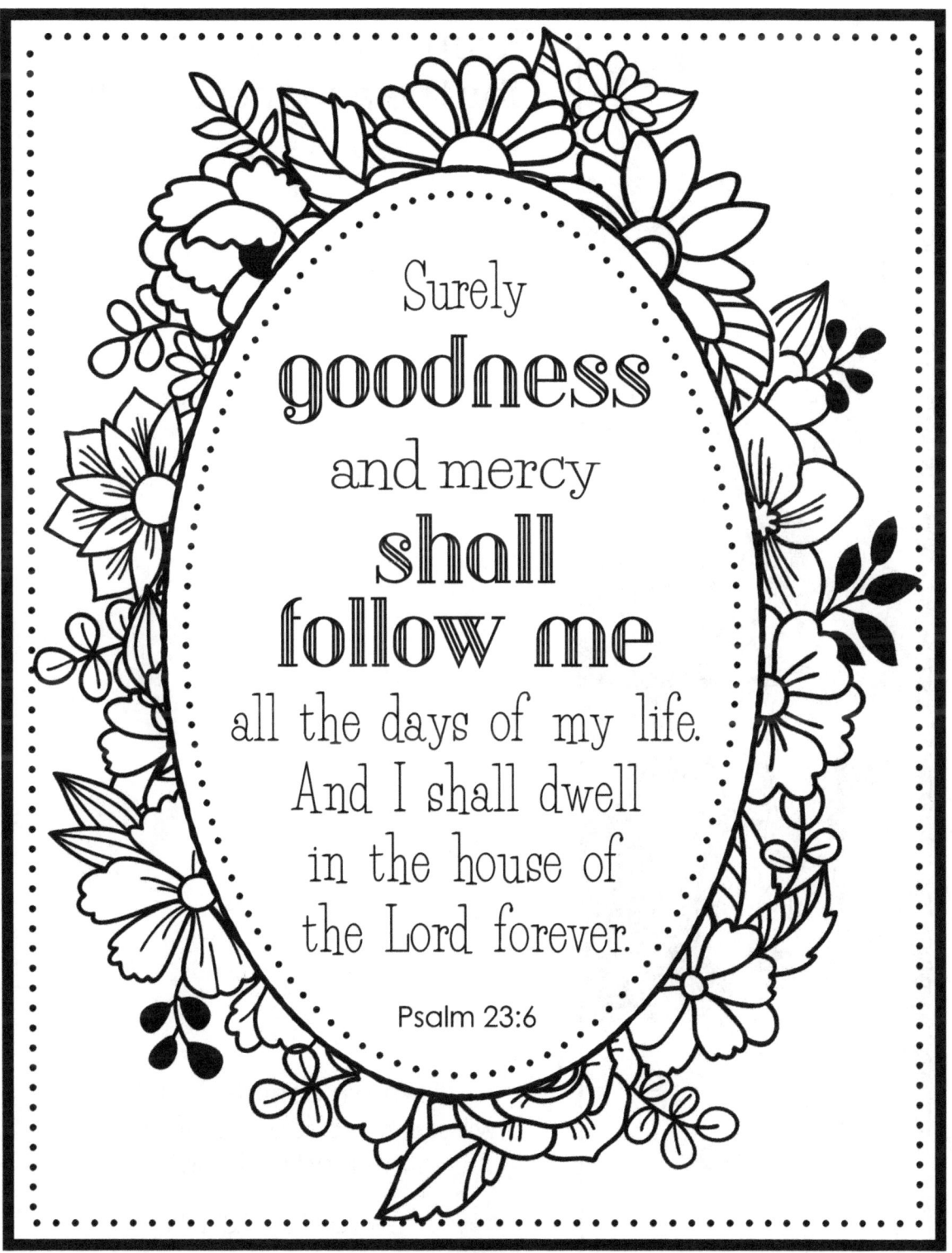

Keep my eyes ever open for the goodness of God

"I remain confident of this:
I will see the goodness of the LORD
in the land of the living."

- Psalm 27:13, NIV

Let my mouth ever sing of His goodness to me

"They celebrate
Your abundant goodness and
joyfully sing of Your righteousness."

- Psalm 145:7, NIV

Be imitators of God, therefore, as beloved children.

- Ephesians 5:1

"But I say to you who hear, love your enemies,
do good to those who hate you, bless those who curse you,
pray for those who mistreat you."

- Luke 6:27-28, NASB

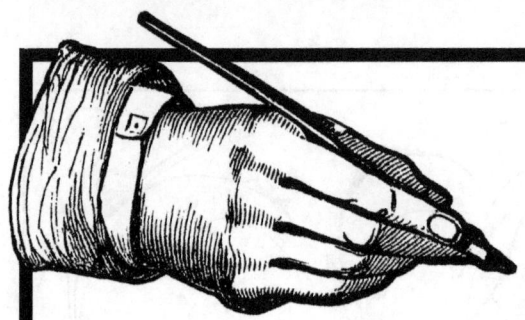

Lord, fill me with goodness

"I myself am convinced, my brothers and sisters, that you yourselves are full of goodness, filled with knowledge and competent to instruct one another."

- Romans 15:14, NIV

Has my faith led to goodness & knowledge?

"For this very reason, make every effort to add to your faith goodness; and to goodness, knowledge…"

- 2 Peter 1:5, NIV

God's Word equips us for every good work

"All Scripture is inspired by God and profitable for teaching, for reproof, for correction, for training in righteousness; so that the man of God may be adequate, equipped for every good work."

- 2 Timothy 3:16-17, NASB

God has provided every good thing and supplied all our needs

"Every good thing given and every perfect gift is from above, coming down from the Father of lights, with whom there is no variation or shifting shadow."

- James 1:17, NASB

Look for ways to do good

"...be ready for every good deed..."

- Titus 3:1, NASB

Plant good deeds & cultivate a good heart

"Let your light so shine before men, that they may
see your good works and glorify your Father in heaven."

- Matthew 5:16, NKJV

Forever Faithful

What the Bible says about faithfulness:

- Psalm 111:7

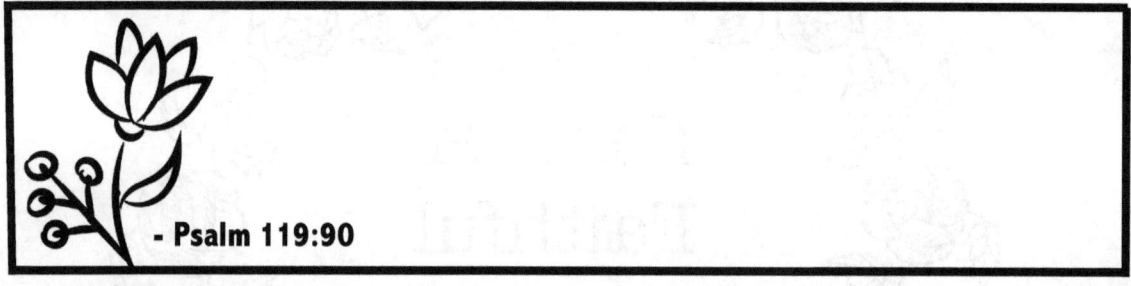
- Psalm 119:90

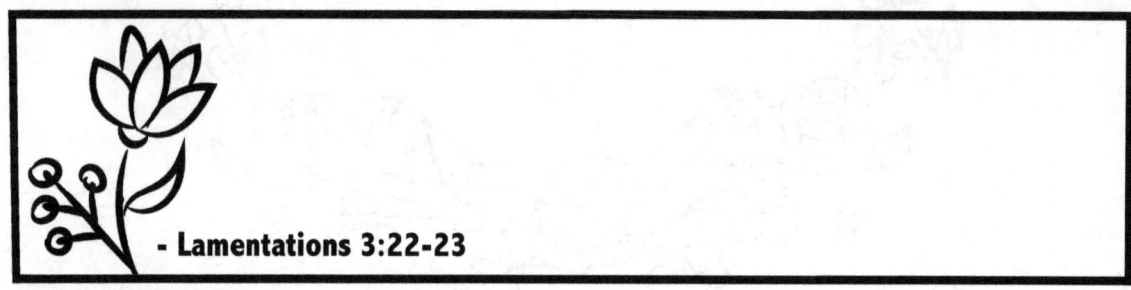
- Lamentations 3:22-23

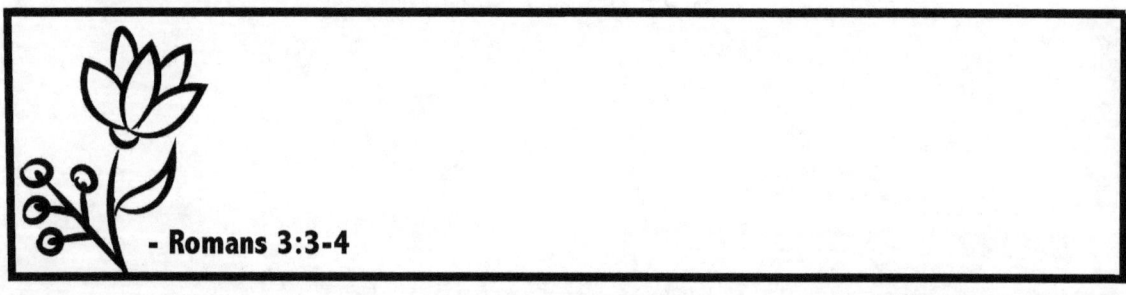
- Romans 3:3-4

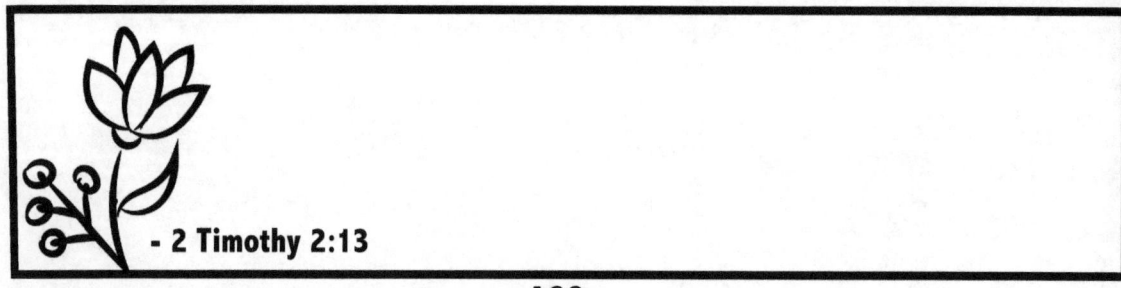
- 2 Timothy 2:13

May all who come behind us find us faithful

"Please, O LORD, remember how I have walked before You faithfully and with wholehearted devotion; I have done what is good in Your sight."

- 2 Kings 20:3, NIV

"For we walk by faith, not by sight."
2 Corinthians 5:7 ESV

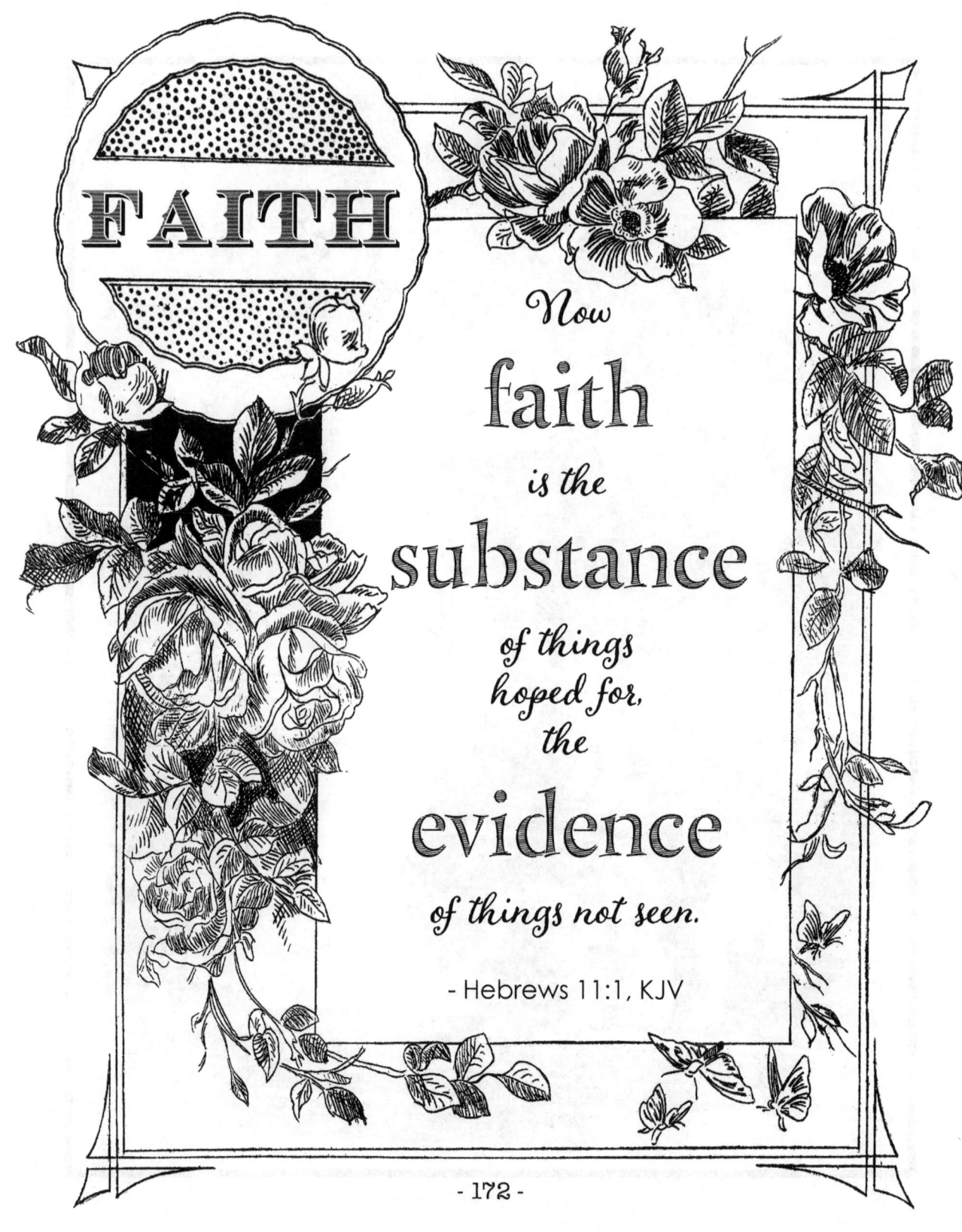

From age to age, He is the same

"It is fitting to proclaim Your loyal love in the morning, and Your faithfulness during the night."

- Psalm 92:1-2, NET

LORD,
YOU ARE MY GOD;
I WILL EXALT YOU
AND
PRAISE YOUR NAME,
FOR IN

PERFECT FAITHFULNESS

YOU HAVE DONE
WONDERFUL THINGS,
THINGS PLANNED
LONG AGO.

- Isaiah 25:1, NIV

God faithfully watches over His own

"For He guards the course of the just
and protects the way of His faithful ones."

- Proverbs 2:8, NIV

I will sing of God's faithfulness to all generations

"I will sing of the LORD's great love forever; with my mouth I will make Your faithfulness known through all generations."

- Psalm 89:1, NIV

I will proclaim
God's faithful love
forever and ever

"I will declare that Your love stands firm forever,
that You have established Your faithfulness in heaven itself."

- Psalm 89:2, NIV

I want to be
a faithful servant of God

"He will guard the feet of His faithful servants,
but the wicked will be silenced in the place of darkness.
'It is not by strength that one prevails.'"

- 1 Samuel 2:9, NIV

I want to keep a short account of wrongs

"If we confess our sins, He is faithful and just and will forgive us our sins and purify us from all unrighteousness."

- 1 John 1:9, NIV

"He is the Rock, His works are perfect, and all His ways are just. A faithful God who does no wrong, upright and just is He."

- Deuteronomy 32:4, NIV

Gentle Strength

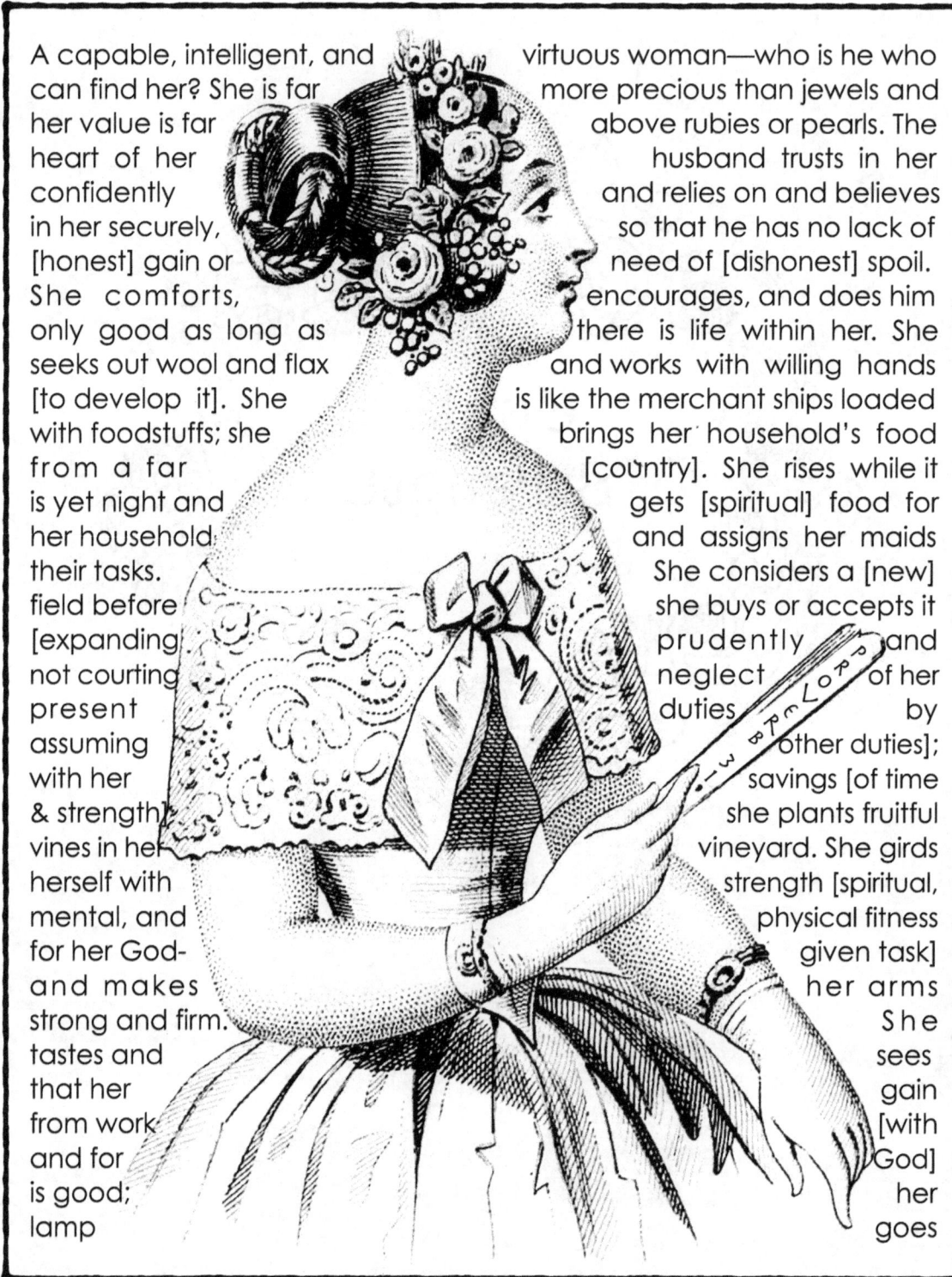

A capable, intelligent, and virtuous woman—who is he who can find her? She is far more precious than jewels and her value is far above rubies or pearls. The heart of her husband trusts in her and relies on and believes confidently in her securely, so that he has no lack of [honest] gain or need of [dishonest] spoil. She comforts, encourages, and does him only good as long as there is life within her. She seeks out wool and flax and works with willing hands [to develop it]. She is like the merchant ships loaded with foodstuffs; she brings her household's food from a far [country]. She rises while it is yet night and gets [spiritual] food for her household and assigns her maids their tasks. She considers a [new] field before she buys or accepts it [expanding prudently and not courting neglect of her present duties by assuming other duties]; with her savings [of time & strength] she plants fruitful vines in her vineyard. She girds herself with strength [spiritual, mental, and physical fitness for her God-given task] and makes her arms strong and firm. She tastes and sees that her gain from work [with and for God] is good; her lamp goes

not out, but it burns on continually through the night [of trouble, privation, or sorrow, warning away fear, doubt, and distrust]. She lays her hands to the spindle, and her hands hold the distaff. She opens her hand to the poor, yes, she reaches out her filled hands to the needy [whether in body, mind, or spirit]. She fears not the snow for her family, for all her household are doubly clothed in scarlet. She makes for herself coverlets, cushions and rugs of tapestry. Her clothing is of linen, pure and fine, and of purple [such as that of which the clothing of the priests & the hallowed cloths of the temple were made]. Her husband is known in the [city's] gates, when he sits among the elders of the land. She makes fine linen garments & leads others to buy them; she delivers to the merchants girdles [or sashes that free one up for service]. Strength and dignity are her clothing & her position is strong and secure; she rejoices over the future [the latter day or time to come knowing that she & her family are in readiness for it]! She opens her mouth in skillful and godly Wisdom, & on her tongue is the law of kindness. She looks well to how things go in her household, & the bread of idleness she won't eat. Her children rise up & bless her & her husband praise her: 'Many daughters've done well, but you excel them all.' Charm is deceptive, and beauty is vain, but a woman who fears the Lord, she shall be praised!

Christ is meek and gentle

"Take My yoke upon you and learn from Me,
for I am gentle and humble in heart,
and you will find rest for your souls."

- Matthew 11:29

Your beauty should not
come from outward adornment,
such as elaborate hairstyles
and the wearing of
gold jewelry or fine clothes.
Rather,
it should be that of your inner self,
the unfading beauty of a

gentle and quiet spirit,

which is of great worth
in God's sight.

- 1 Peter 3:3-4, NIV

What the Bible says about gentleness:

- James 3:17

- 2 Tim. 2:25

- 1 Tim. 3:2-4

- Prov. 15:1

- Gal. 5:22-23

Gentle is as gentle does

Use gentle speech...

"A gentle answer turns away wrath,
but a harsh word stirs up anger."

- Proverbs 15:1, NIV

...and a calm voice

"If the anger of the ruler flares up against you, do not resign from your position, for a calm response can undo great offenses."

- Ecclesiastes 10:4, NET

"The wicked are trapped by their own words, but the godly escape such trouble. Wise words bring many benefits, and hard work brings rewards."

- Proverbs 12:13-14, NLT

I must choose my words wisely

"Gentle words are a tree of life;
a deceitful tongue crushes the spirit."

- Proverbs 15:4, NLT

How can I help the weak?

"Now we who are strong ought to bear the weaknesses of those without strength and not just please ourselves."

- Romans 15;1, NASB

What the Bible says about strength:

 - Philippians 4:13

 - Isaiah 40:30-31

 - Exodus 15:2

 - Eph. 3:16-18

 - Psalm 28:7-8

When I am weak...

"But He said to me,
"My grace is sufficient for you,
for My power
is made perfect in weakness."
Therefore I will boast
all the more gladly
about my weaknesses,
so that Christ's power
may rest on me."

- 2 Corinthians 12:9, NIV

... then I am strong.

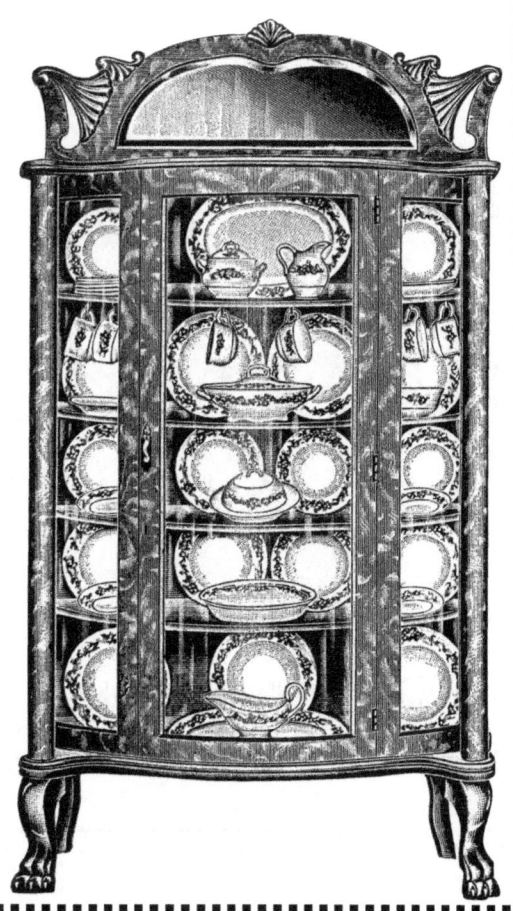

"That is why, for Christ's sake,
I delight in weaknesses,
in insults, in hardships,
in persecutions, in difficulties.
For when I am weak,
then I am strong."

- 2 Corinthians 12:10, NIV

"Let your gentleness be evident to all. The Lord is near."

- Philippians 4:5, NIV

Self-Control

What the Bible says about self-control:

- 1 Corinthians 9:24-25

- Galatians 5:22-23

- 1 Peter 1:5-7

- Proverbs 13:3

Self-control is a protection

"A man without self-control is like a city broken into and left without walls."

- Proverbs 25:28, ESV

Better to be **patient** than powerful; better to have **self-control** than to conquer a city.

— Prov. 16:32, NLT

Studying Scripture
will help me discipline my mind...

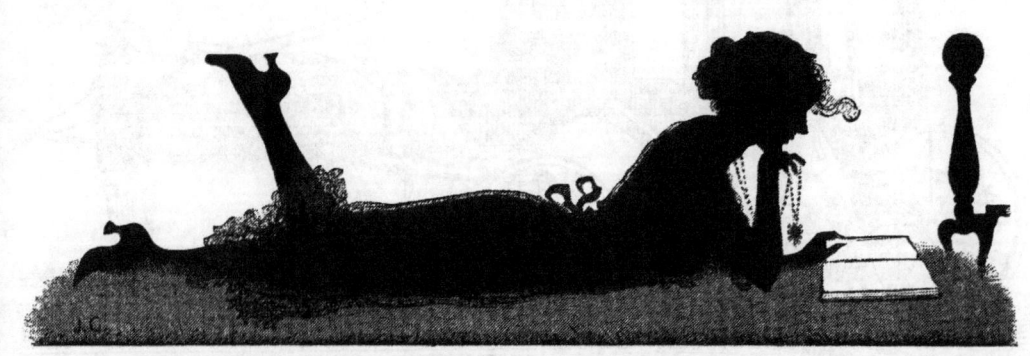

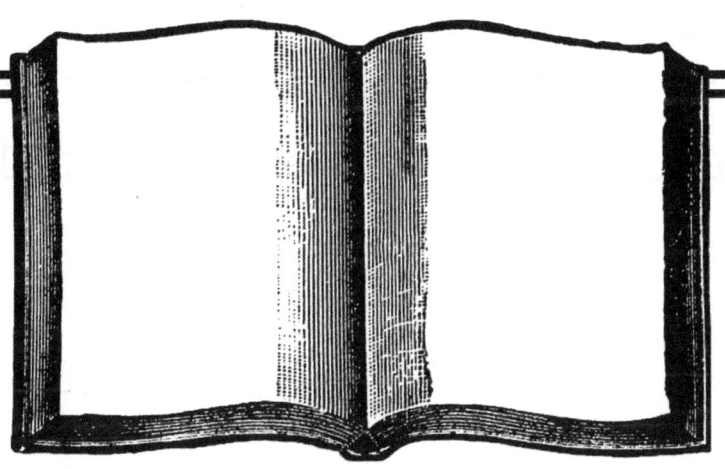

...and take control of my thoughts

"We destroy arguments and every lofty opinion
raised against the knowledge of God, and
take every thought captive to obey Christ."

- 2 Corinthians 10:5, ESV

Modesty never goes out of style

"Likewise also women should adorn
themselves in respectable apparel,
with modesty and self-control,
not with braided hair or gold or pearls
or costly clothing,"

- 1 Timothy 2:9, ESV

How can I exercise more self-discipline?

"But I discipline my body and keep it under control, lest after preaching to others I myself should be disqualified."

- 1 Corinthians 9:27, ESV

Do I listen and think before I speak?

"This you know, my beloved brethren. But everyone must be quick to hear, slow to speak, and slow to anger."

- James 1:19, NASB

Place a guard on my mouth

"If anyone thinks he is religious without controlling his tongue, his religion is useless and he deceives himself."

- James 1;26, CSB

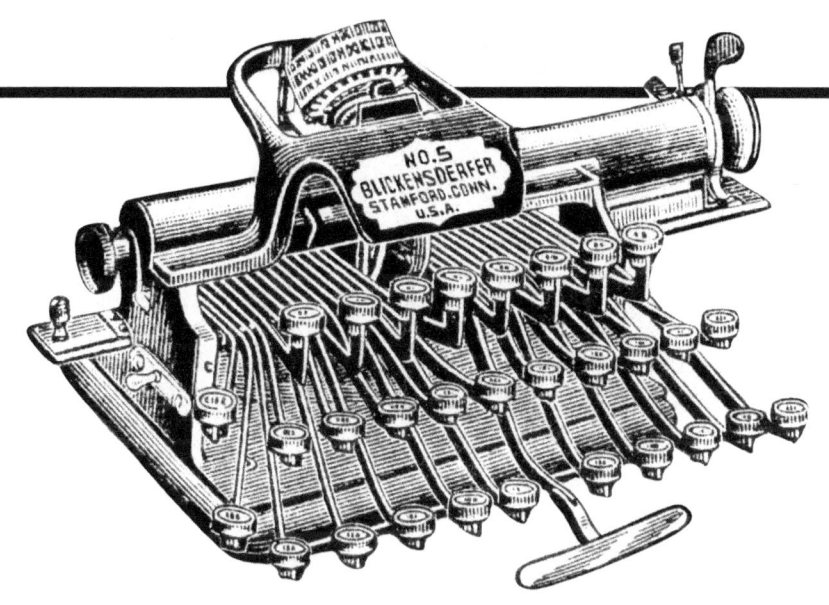

May my words honor God

"For we all stumble in many ways.
If someone does not stumble in what he says,
he is a perfect individual, able to control the entire body as well."

- James 3:2, NET

"The end of all things is near.
You must be self-controlled and alert, to be able to pray."

- 1 Peter 4:7, GNT

Quiet Confidence

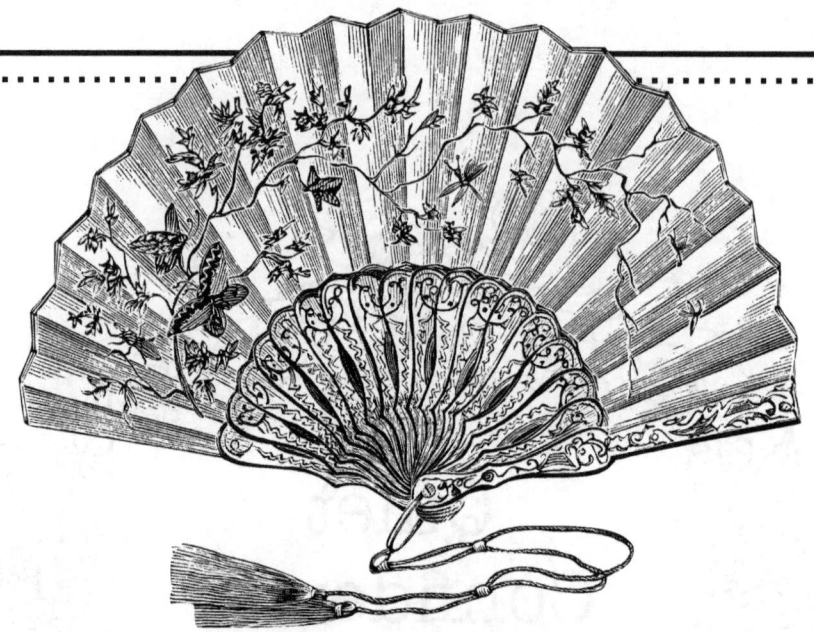

I am confident...

"By this, love is perfected with us,
so that we may have confidence in the day of judgment;
because as He is, so also are we in this world."

- 1 John 4:17, NASB

...He will come for me

"And now, dear children,
continue in Him, so that when He appears we may be
confident & unashamed before Him at His coming."

- 1 John 2:28, NIV

Proverbs 3:5-6

Trust in the LORD with all thine heart; and lean not unto thine own understanding. In all thy ways acknowledge Him, and He shall direct thy paths.

We can be confident following God's direction

"In the fear of the LORD *there is* strong confidence, And His children will have a place of refuge."

- Proverbs 14:26, NKJV

Still hard at work

"For I am confident of this very thing, that He who began a good work in you will perfect it until the day of Christ Jesus."

- Philippians 1:6, NASB

Growing in virtue

"Who can find a virtuous woman?
for her price *is* far above rubies.
Her husband has full confidence in her
and lacks nothing of value."

- Proverbs 31:10-11, KJV, NIV

How accurately does my life reflect Christ?

"For now we see in a mirror dimly, but then face to face; now I know in part, but then I will know fully just as I also have been fully known."

- 1 Corinthians 13:12, NASB

What the Bible says about confidence:

- Isaiah 32:17

- 2 Corinthians 3:4-5

- Philippians 3:7-9

- Psalm 20:7-8

- Hebrews 6:9-10

Our privileged life

"Because of our faith,
Christ has brought us into this place of undeserved privilege where we now stand, and we confidently and joyfully look forward to sharing God's glory."

- Romans 5:2, NLT

Everything we have comes from God

"Let the one who boasts boast in the Lord."

- 2 Cor. 10:17, NIV

Our efforts fail without His blessing

"Let the beauty of the LORD our God be upon us, and establish the work of our hands for us; yes, establish the work of our hands."

- Psalm 90:17

Have faith in God

"But blessed is the one who trusts in the Lord, whose confidence is in Him."

- Jeremiah 17:7, NIV

The future is His

"Do not boast about tomorrow,
for you do not know
what a day may bring."

- Proverbs 27:1, NIV

"The fruit of that righteousness will be peace;
its effect will be quietness and confidence forever."

- Isaiah 32:17

Freedom of Choice

What the Bible says about choices we make:

- Proverbs 4:10-15

- Deut. 30:15-19

- Proverbs 18:21

- James 4:6-10

- Proverbs 14:1-2

I can choose to be patient

"Behold, as the eyes of servants look to the hand of their master,
As the eyes of a maid to the hand of her mistress,
So our eyes look to the LORD our God, Until He is gracious to us."

- Psalm 123:2, NASB

I can choose to be helpful

"We urge you, brethren, admonish the unruly, encourage the fainthearted, help the weak, be patient with everyone."

1 Thessalonians 5:14, NASB

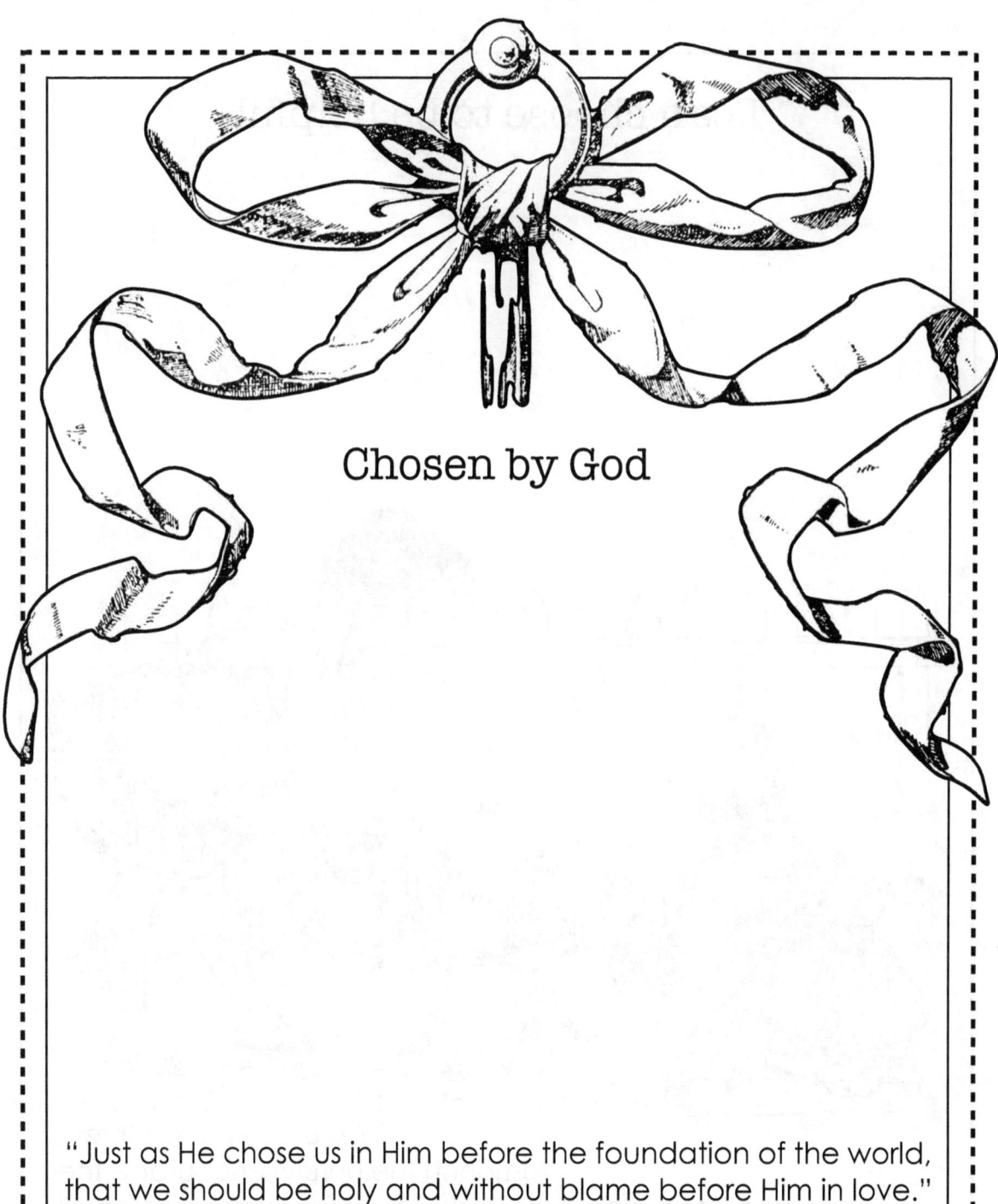

Chosen by God

"Just as He chose us in Him before the foundation of the world, that we should be holy and without blame before Him in love."

- Ephesians 1:4, NKJV

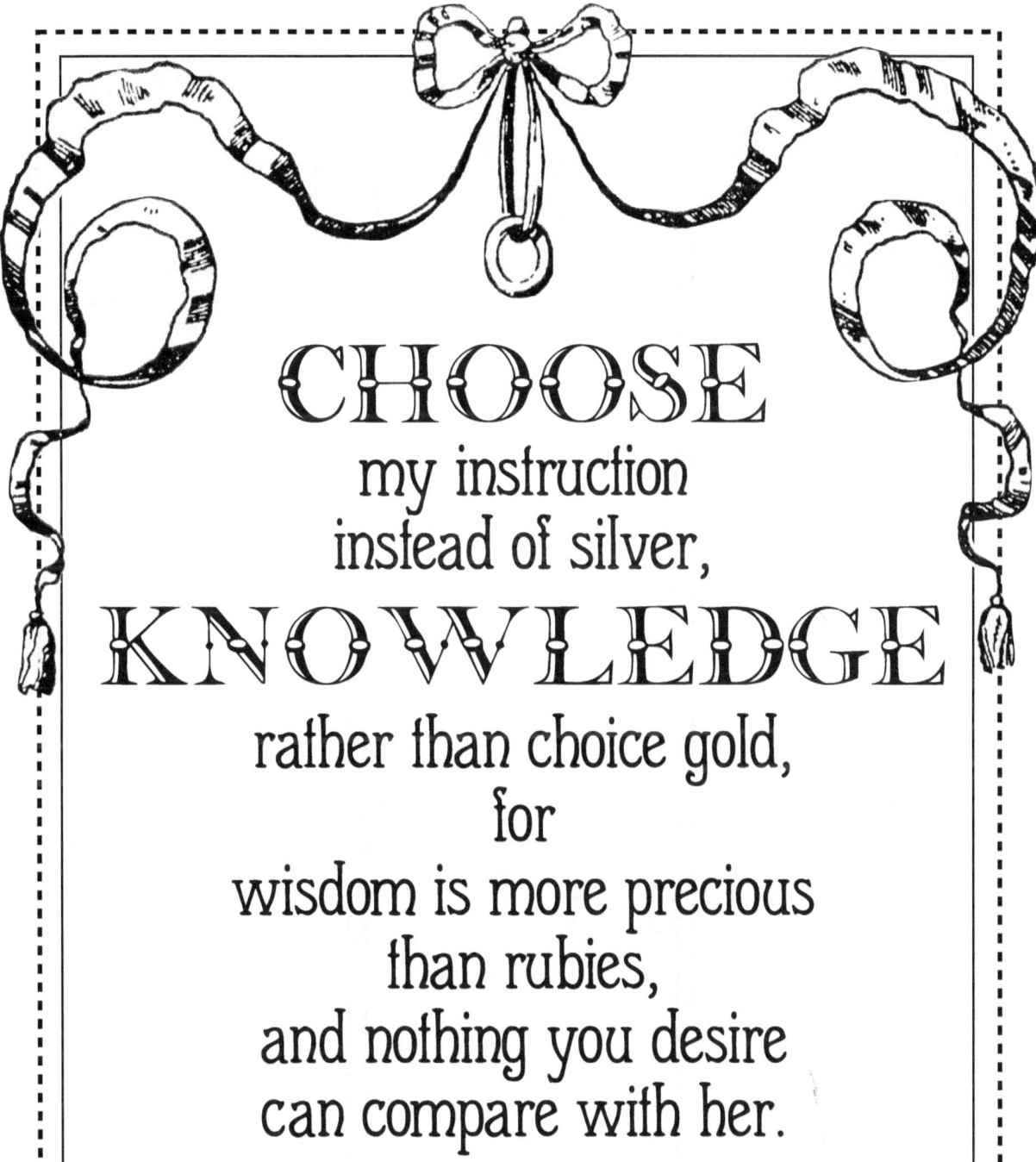

CHOOSE my instruction instead of silver, **KNOWLEDGE** rather than choice gold, for wisdom is more precious than rubies, and nothing you desire can compare with her.

- Proverbs 8:10-11, NIV

- Proverbs 1:7 -

- Romans 11:22 -

- Matthew 7:24-27 -

- Proverbs 1:29-31 -

- Romans 6:16-18 -

- Jeremiah 17:10 -

We must walk the walk, not just talk the talk

"For it is not those who hear the law who are righteous in God's sight, but it is those who obey the law who will be declared righteous."

- Romans 2:13, NIV

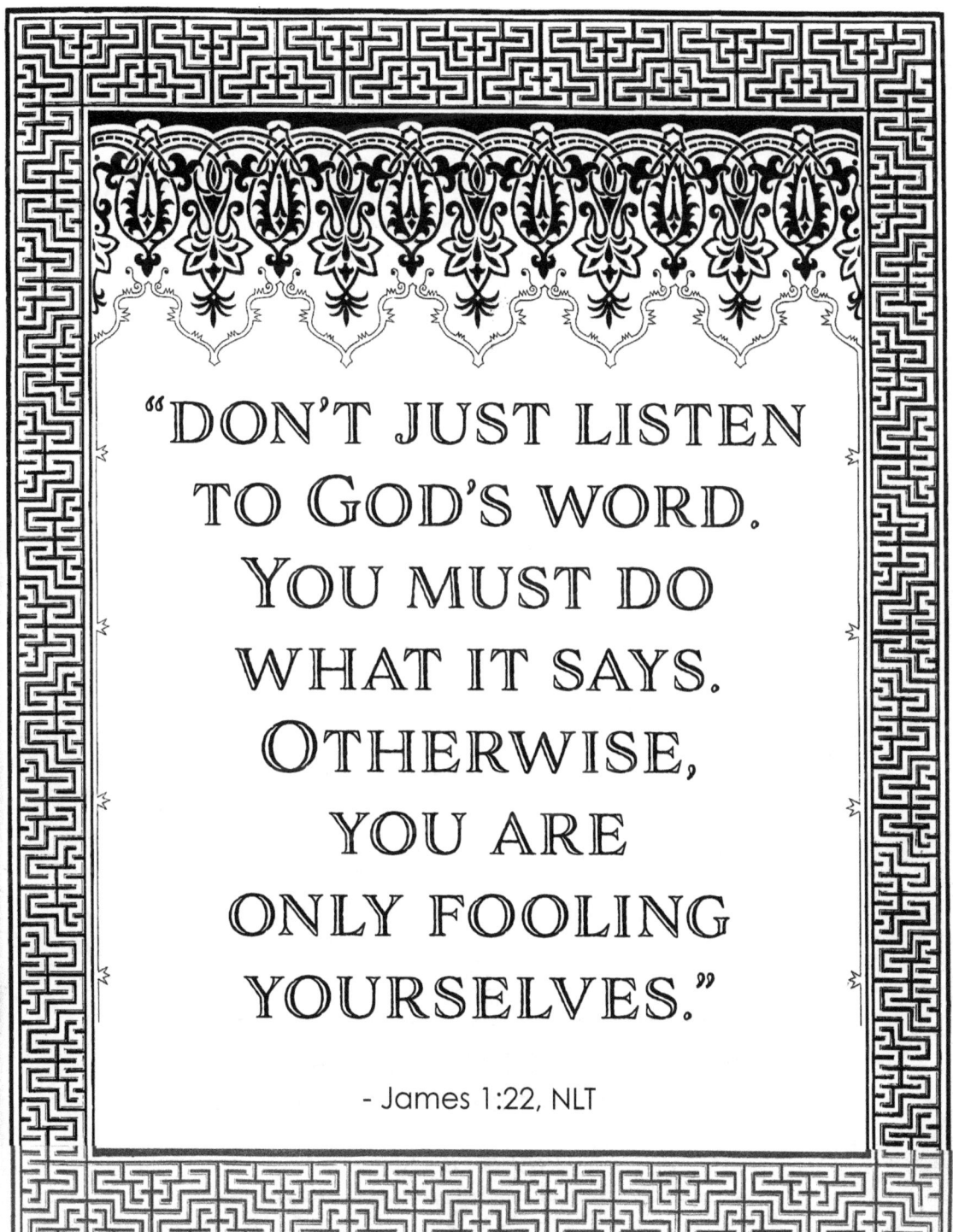

"Don't just listen to God's word. You must do what it says. Otherwise, you are only fooling yourselves."

- James 1:22, NLT

"The eyes of the LORD *are* in every place,
Keeping watch on the evil and the good."

- Proverbs 15:3

One Last Word from the Author:

I hope you've enjoyed working your way through this book as much as I enjoyed creating it. I've been making and keeping personal journals and sketchbooks—and lots and lots of scrapbooks—for over 45 years now, so creating this series for others to use has been a lot of fun. I made the books with my own children in mind, as they definitely take after their mom when it comes to writing and drawing, but I thought perhaps other people (young or old) might like them, as well.

If that describes you, I would love for you to leave a positive review on Amazon, so other readers can get an idea of what the journal is like. Additional volumes are available—including journals for boys, moms, and wives—on a variety of topics. If you have any questions or suggestions, feel free to contact me through my family's website, www.flandersfamily.info. Although I read every message I receive, time constraints do not allow me to respond personally to most of them. My 12 kids and 12 grandkids (so far!) keep me much too busy for that, at least in this season of my life!

Check out my other books:

25 Ways to Communicate Respect to Your Husband:
A Handbook for Wives

Love Your Husband/Love Yourself:
Embracing God's Purpose for Passion in Marriage

Get Up & Go:
Fun Ideas for Getting Fit as a Family

Sit Down & Eat:
Fun Ideas for Making Mealtime Memorable

Pack Up & Leave:
Travel Tips for Fun Family Vacations

Balance:
The Art of Minding What Matters Most

Glad Tidings:
25 Years of Flanders Family Christmas Letters

And my full line of coloring books:

Color the Word: The Bread of Life

Color the Word: Clothed in His Righteousness

Color the Word: The Fruit of the Spirit

Color the Word: My Heart, Thy Home

Color the Word: The Walk of Faith

Don't miss the other volumes in this series:

www.ingramcontent.com/pod-product-compliance
Lightning Source LLC
LaVergne TN
LVHW061331060426
835512LV00013B/2603